advance praise for

Beneath the Mask

"This book is an invaluable contribution to our understanding of the developmental challenges and psychological issues that adopted adolescents and their families experience. It offers critically needed insights into effective therapeutic work with adopted adolescents and is enriched with specific techniques, tools, and illustrative case examples. Mental health professionals who work with adopted adolescents and their families will find it to be an essential resource to be read and consulted time and time again."

— *Madelyn Freundlich, Director of Policy, Children's Rights*

"This book is of enormous clinical relevance and application to a particular child population that has been too-long forgotten. The authors systematically explore both the intrapsychic and social factors that complicate the development pathway of adopted children. This book is a must-read for novice and experienced clinicians."

— *Kirkland C. Vaughans, Ph.D., Editor of*
Journal of Infant, Child, and Adolescent Psychotherapy

"This book is a welcome addition to literature in the adoption field and is a must-read. It is interesting and filled with case examples and poetry that demonstrate the authors' deep experience working with teen-adopted persons. It is replete with practical suggestions of therapeutic interventions."

— *Sharon Kaplan Roszia, M.S., Program Director of special needs adoptions for the Kinship Center of southern California, adoptive parent, author, and social worker*

"The most powerful feature of *Beneath the Mask: Understanding Adopted Teens* is the wealth of specific, concrete suggestions for dealing with issues like rejection, depression, secrecy, and identity confusion. The authors' clinical insights are presented through multiple case examples that illustrate clinical assessment, work with parents, individual psychotherapy, and group therapy. This book will be most helpful to mental health professionals... It should also broaden the understanding of adoptive parents and guide them in the selection of knowledgeable therapists for their families.

— *William Bernet, M.D., Director of Forensic Psychiatry,*
Vanderbilt Medical Center.

"After years of working with adoptive families as a caseworker, I have come to know that finding just the right mental health provider — one who has adoption expertise and who is humble in the face of the challenges adoptive families often face — can literally make or break the continuation of the placement and the integrity of the family. I am delighted, therefore, to find this book, *Beneath the Mask: Understanding Adopted Teens*, which carefully and clearly teaches therapists and counselors what they really need to know before jumping in — especially those who decide to work with adolescent adoptees!"

— *Barb Holtan, MA, MSW, Executive Director,*
Adoption Exchange Association

Beneath the MASK

Beneath the
MASK

THE CENTER FOR ADOPTION SUPPORT & EDUCATION

understanding
Adopted Teens

Case Studies & Treatment Considerations
for Therapists & Parents

Debbie Riley, LCMFT, with John Meeks, M.D.

Silver Spring, MD

Beneath the Mask: Understanding Adopted Teens
by Debbie Riley, LCMFT, with John Meeks, M.D.

Published by C.A.S.E. Publications
4000 Blackburn Lane, Suite 260, Burtonsville, MD 20866
For ordering information, visit: www.adoptionsupport.org.

Authors have used case examples to highlight clinical and treatment issues. To protect the confidentiality of the individuals, names and circumstances have been altered unless otherwise requested. Clients whose work is included have reviewed transcripts, approved all artwork and poetry, and provided written permission.

Cover mask photography by Jane Credille, Pneuma Books, LLC. Cover and interior design by Pneuma Books, LLC. For more info, visit www. pneumabooks.com

Printed in the United States of America by United Graphics, Inc.

16 15   7 6 5 4

Publisher's Cataloging-In-Publication
(Prepared by The Donohue Group)

Riley, Debbie B.
   Beneath the mask : understanding adopted teens : case studies & treatment considerations for therapists & parents / Debbie Riley with John Meeks.

   p. : ill. ; cm.
   ISBN-13: 978-0-9711732-2-4
   ISBN-10: 0-9711732-2-2

1. Adoption—Psychological aspects.   2. Adopted children—Psychological aspects.   3. Adopted children—Family relationships.   4. Adoption—Case studies.   5. Teenagers—Counseling of—Handbooks, manuals, etc.   I. Meeks, John E.

HV875 .R55 2004
362.734   LCCN: 2004116576

Dedicated to my son Sean —
the joy of my life.

Table of contents

foreword
by Dr. Joyce Maguire Pavao

I can't recall which famous psychoanalyst said that adolescence is the closest thing to psychosis, but every human being who has lived through adolescence knows this has many shades of truth and resonance. For adopted adolescents, the challenges of building an identity while struggling with mystery — and often trauma — are even more complex. No matter what the circumstances into which a child is born or the type of adoption one ends up with, the foundational experience of the adopted person involves loss and transition.

Needless to say, by the time the adopted child reaches the teen years, there are additional issues and concerns that are a part of the already complex work of being an adolescent in our culture. It is evident to those of us who have worked in the field of adoption that adopted adolescents and their families face some core challenges. My models for treatment and training, developed over the past thirty years, and used widely by those I have trained, state that there are normative crises in adoption and that many things that appear to be "a bit different" are often normal under the circumstances of adoption. A few of those normative crises are the extraordinary struggle to understand identity, often including racial, ethnic, cultural and class identity; the feeling of belonging but not belonging; and the issue of abandonment.

Riley and Meeks' book is a much-needed look into the lives of these children, and it is a template for professionals to develop strategies and skills to help these young people to heal and to grow.

Included are descriptive examples of the presenting problems of these teens and their families, as well as specific recommendations for therapeutic techniques. The authors give professionals access to the many areas of expertise that are needed to effectively serve this complex population, including the sensitivity and awareness that will help to prevent therapists from pathologizing some of the behaviors and feelings that are very common and normative to this population.

I would recommend this book for any professional who works with adolescent adopted people and their families. It is essential that professionals are not only sensitive to the issues in adoptive families but competent to help teens and their families work through them. *Beneath the Mask: Understanding Adopted Teens* is an opportunity to observe some excellent techniques and exposure to psycho-education that will be beneficial to parents as well as to professionals.

Unfortunately, professionals can sometimes hurt, more than help, the adopted teens and their families when they expect the worst and label teens with whatever the current designer diagnosis is. Recently a mom came into my office to tell me that she had read a description of bipolar disorder on the Web, and she was sure that her thirteen-year-old daughter had this diagnosis. I have known this child since she was five, and I assure you she is not bipolar (any more than all thirteen year olds appear to be!). This mother fell into a trap that many professionals fall into when working with adopted adolescents.

The more we pathologize and clump adopted teens into boxes of diagnoses, the more we neglect to treat the underlying issues of loss and identity confusion. A family-systems perspective along with a psycho-dynamic approach is the best combination of techniques for getting a clear view of these amazing teens and their complex families. For that reason, this book will prove to be an invaluable resource for the therapist, who encounters adopted adolescents and their families.

Dr. Joyce Maguire Pavao
Pavao Consulting and Coaching
Pre/Post Adoption Consulting and Training (PACT)
kinnect@gmail.com
www.joycemaguirepavao.com
Author of *The Family of Adoption*, Beacon Press (1998 and 2004)

preface

Much has been written over the years about the reasons why practitioners might want to steer clear of teens in their clinical practices. It is well understood that adolescent attitudes might be dangerous to the health of your dignity. Fortunately or unfortunately, I never heeded the warnings and have focused my clinical career of the past thirty years to providing therapeutic services to those sometimes uncontrollable, unmanageable, histrionic, oppositional and often-defiant beings we call adolescents. For the past eighteen years I have had Dr. John Meeks as my colleague and mentor in this questionable adventure. Dr. Meeks is the author of *The Fragile Alliance*, perhaps the first book to tell it like it is in describing the encounter with a real live adolescent in psychotherapy. For that reason, the book has had an extended success and is in its fifth edition.

Dr. Meeks and I have worked together in inpatient psychiatric settings, outpatient dual-diagnosis programs for adolescents and special educational schools for emotionally disturbed adolescents. During the first five years of our collaboration we both treated many adopted teens but never fully embraced them as a unique clinical population in need of special consideration.

Over thirteen years ago I became interested in adoption both from a professional and personal perspective. My husband and I became adoptive parents and I grew increasingly curious about the issues inherent in adoption. This personal experience heightened my sensitivity to the numbers of adopted children and teens with whom I had previously worked in a variety of clinical settings: outpatient mental health clinics, impatient psychiatric hospitals, juvenile justice arenas, residential treatment centers, and specialized schools for children with learning and emotional disabilities.

Questions started to well up in my mind. I began to ask myself why there were so many adopted teens in these settings. Did being adopted place the adolescent at special risk for a myriad of psychiatric problems? If so, what were the psychological risks of adoption? Why did it appear that these children also had higher incidences of referrals to special educational settings? Why were they overrepresented in the juvenile justice system?

I began to look at some of the research, which reflected that a larger proportion of adopted adolescents received mental health services than their nonadopted peers. Recent comprehensive reviews reported that adopted adolescents receiving mental health services ranged from 5 to 17 percent (Miller et al. 2000), although they only represent 2 percent of the population. In regard to the educational needs of this population, research indicates that adopted children have higher incidences of learning disabilities, academic problems, and difficulties with attentional issues. (Brodzinsky and Steiger, 1991) Several explanations have been offered. Some researchers noted that the higher socioeconomic and educational status of adoptive parents afforded them the ability and the means to identify mild or developing problems in their adopted children and to pay for counseling.

Others contended that because adoptive parents had interfaced with social service agencies to facilitate the adoption process, they were more comfortable than nonadoptive parents to access support services through a social service agency. They called this a "lower threshold for referral" (Miller, op. cit.). Others did not credit adoptive parents with early identification of problems but suggested that adoptive parents may be more anxious than biological parents when it relates to problematic behaviors. This view would suggest that some adopted children are referred for mental health care unnecessarily. None of these viewpoints has been proven, and the fact remains that adopted children present for treatment at a high rate and practitioners find their problems all too real.

In view of these facts, I wondered why practitioners, including myself, were so lax about focusing on the adoption experience with the teens and their parents. Why didn't we include questions on psycho-social history forms and intake / assessments documents about adoption? Why did we ignore the fact that adoption is a circumstance of emotional importance that affects the adopted person and his or her family throughout their lives?

All this questioning led me to study the field of adoption. I reviewed the literature and dialogued with pioneers in the field. This review led me to the conclusion that adoption *is* a highly significant emotional event in the psychological development of teens. It is during the adolescent period that most adopted persons first clearly recognize the unique issues that will continue to be processed throughout their lives. This emerging recognition of their unique family situation has a powerful impact on family relationships, identity formation, and the achievement of individuation and independence.

In spite of the vital importance of this struggle, I came to embrace the reality that there were few specialized centers to provide mental health services to adoptive families and a shortage of providers who were adequately trained to help. This did not make sense to me given what the research was saying regarding the overwhelming needs of this clinical population.

Within myself I felt a growing pull to respond to the challenge. I was fortunate in 1998 to have the opportunity to find the financial and professional support to plan and implement an adoptive family support center — The Center for Adoption Support and Education Inc., generally known as C.A.S.E. The goal of C.A.S.E. is to strengthen the well-being of adopted children and their families. We achieve our mission by

1. providing a safe place for adoptees of all ages to share their thoughts and feelings about adoption;
2. promoting the mental health of adoptees and their families through specialized pre- and post-adoption counseling services;
3. educating families, professionals, and the community about the unique joys and challenges of adoption;
4. establishing collaborations and partnerships within the public and private sectors; and
5. participating in the national and international field of adoption study, research, and program development.

C.A.S.E is one of a few nonplacement centers in the country that exists exclusively to provide clinical, educational, and supportive services to adoptive families and their children from all adoptive experiences. Over the past fifteen years, professionals at C.A.S.E. have treated thousands of adoptive families and their children. Our clients include children and teens from agency adoptions, private adoption, and international adoption. Our clients are children and teens from the United States to China and everywhere in between. We have served children placed at birth and children adopted when they were older — sometimes *much* older. All of the youngsters with later adoptions have had extensive contact with domestic child welfare systems or with orphanages in foreign countries.

No matter what their adoption experience was, there appeared to be some commonalities among all the adolescents. They all ponder why they were "given up" for adoption; they have deep-seated thoughts and feelings about their birth parents, whether they had a prior relationship or not; and at some point in time, even for a fleeting minute, they have all wondered what they did to cause the relinquishment and were conflicted as to how to talk about this with their parents.

Given my thirty years of experience treating this age group, I became the in-house expert in adolescence by default. I have worked with and supervised the clinical services to hundreds of adopted teens. I have had the honor of joining many of them in their journey as they try to figure out the significance of their adoption and the impact it now has upon their identity and future.

If you are thinking that this must not be an easy journey, you are right. It is not easy for the young people, and it is not easy for the adoptive parents. I am constantly asked questions like these by frightened and confused adoptive parents: "What's wrong here?" "Am I doing something wrong?" "Is the problem a result of adoption?" "How does being adopted affect my son/daughter?" "They seem to be confused about who they are. Is adolescence harder for them because they are adopted?" "Did we make a terrible mistake for them and for us?"

Behind these questions is the fear that the adopted adolescent will begin to reevaluate their adoption and reject the love, affection, and parenting they accepted when they were younger. As these worries diminish in therapy, they are replaced by equally troubling but more productive concerns. Now the parents say, "I wish I had more information for them." Or, "I feel horrible that we don't have much to share with them!" The parents ask, "How can we help? What can we do?"

Concurrently I sit with the pain of the teens who are searching for answers to their questions. They wonder, "Why did my mother leave me? Was there something wrong with me?" Or they ask, "Who was my birth father? What did he look like? Did he mean anything to my birth mother? If I could only ask them why! I wish I knew someone who looked like me!" In addition to experiencing this pain, they worry that their interest in birth parents is disloyal to their adoptive parents. They also worry about society's attitudes about their family situation. "Other kids get embarrassed when they learn I'm adopted." Or conversely, "Why do people always ask me so many questions about my adoption — I'm sick of it!"

All these years later and still I review case files that indicate a lack of adoption-focused therapy and a resulting lack of improvement. Tragically, sometimes placements are disrupted because parents could not see the light at the end of the tunnel. My heart breaks when families and teens come in and reveal that they have seen multiple therapists who never asked about adoption or seemed comfortable talking about it.

The parents seem to know intuitively that somewhere in this complex maze adoption plays a role in the issues confronting their son or daughter and that they need help in unraveling the web. That was the source of this book. The impetus behind my decision to organize and record my thoughts and experiences came from the teenagers and parents with whom I have had the privilege and honor to work. They taught me that all of us need a deeper appreciation of the psychological issues inherent in adoption.

This book is written for the therapist, mental health provider, guidance or school counselor, social worker, psychologist, psychiatrist, or pastoral counselor who interfaces with an adopted teen and his or her family. Dr. Meeks and I hope that by sharing our impressions we can give you a framework with which you can deepen your own appreciation of the significance of the adoptive experience. We hope that you will share your thoughts and experiences with us.

We also hope that the book will help adoptive parents, agency personnel, and others directly involved in adoption matters to understand the goals and techniques of therapy. We hope adoptive

Beneath the Mask

parents can use this book as a framework in which to find adoption-competent mental health providers.

The techniques suggested throughout the book are drawn from effective approaches used by therapists at C.A.S.E. The authors are grateful to all the staff members at C.A.S.E. who helped to develop and refine these techniques.

The adolescents' creative writings throughout the book will help to convey the powerful, complex feelings of adopted teens who were able find a safe place in which to explore their personal issues of adoption. It is their tears, anger, sense of bewilderment, and quest to know why that has provided me with whatever may be good in this book.

WHY
BY Elyse

Why did you have to give me up?
Why did you have to leave me?
Why couldn't our family just be?
When will you be able to meet me?

Our goal is to not pathologize adoption. Adoption itself is not the problem; rather it is those inherent variables in adoption that become the underpinnings of the profound complexities of the adoption experience during adolescence. It is important to recognize that the case examples presented in this book are not representative of all adoptions and many were chosen to support the key issues inherent in adopted teens. The majority of adoptees we have worked with have successfully embraced the issues adoption has posed for them and moved forward to lead wonderful, bright, hopeful futures.

I used to think if I hid behind my mask and didn't let people
close to me, I would protect myself from more hurt.
Kayley

secrets, silence and rejection
the adopted adolescent

If a therapist sees adolescent patients, it is likely the therapist will encounter adoptees. In fact, about one third of adolescents referred for psychotherapy are adopted. This finding has been confirmed in several studies. However, only 2 percent of the general population is adopted (Miller et al., 2000). Consider these facts about adoptees and psychotherapy:

- Adolescence is the peak period for psychiatric referrals in the life of the adopted person.

- Adopted younger children and adults enter psychotherapy at a rate much more similar to the general population (Brodzinsky, Smith, and Brodzinsky, 1998).

- School problems and runaway behavior, common reasons for adolescent referral, are more common in the adopted population than in any other part of the youth population. This is true even if adoptees are compared with high-risk populations, such as single-parent families. (Howard and Smith, 2003).

Since the psychotherapist who specializes in treating adolescents is likely to have several adopted youngsters in his or her caseload, proper understanding of common therapeutic traps is important. Most authors agree that adopted children — of all ages — pose significant treatment challenges (Kernberg, 1986; Sherick, 1983; Subramanian, 2004; Zuckerman and Buschsbaum, 2000). Treatment failures are all too frequent. Many therapists are frustrated in their efforts to explore the adopted adolescent's feelings about the complex family structure that he or she inhabits. Why is the task of treating an adolescent so formidable? There are several interlocking reasons:

- The adolescent patient may be unaware of the emotional significance of the adopted status. In fact, if asked about the emotional impact of their adoption, most adolescents deny there are any issues. We discuss the reasons for this bland reaction in chapter 4.

- The therapist may not even be told that the patient is adopted.

- In office practice, adolescents are rarely referred for the express purpose of exploring issues related to their adopted status. They are referred for treatment of school difficulties, acting out behavior, drug involvement, or any of the other presenting complaints common in this developmental period.

At this point, it might be useful to take a brief detour to discuss adolescent treatment in general. Then we'll discuss some of the problems peculiar to the circumstance of growing up adopted.

THE ADOLESCENT IN PSYCHOTHERAPY

Adolescents have always been a source of great interest (and often great concern) to adults in general and, in recent years, to mental health specialists in particular. Opinions about this age group are most often negative. Adolescents are considered disrespectful, rebellious, and secretive. All too often, they are viewed as the source of many community problems, including crimes both petty and dangerous. At other times, such as the 1960s and 1970s, they were presented as seers, wiser than the adults around them and a possible salvation for society's ills.

In any case, there is a tendency to generalize and dramatize the age group. In generation after generation, teens have seized the imagination of adults — with the emphasis on *imagination*! Most often, adolescents are demonized. Dire predictions about their futures abound. Friedenberg summed it up well: "Every major industrial society believes that it has a serious youth problem" (1965). Recent neurological research (Giedd et al., 1999; Sowell et al., 2003) supports the observation that adolescents think differently from adults and reveals that the adolescent's brain function has not fully developed. Historically, society has tended to exaggerate these differences.

Mental health workers have hardly been immune to this tendency. Clinicians form their ideas about adolescents from observing their treatment cases, and early authors described adolescence as a turbulent and troubled time. Even a luminary like Anna Freud suggested that adolescents who appeared well adjusted were merely avoiding the necessary psychic work of the period. She also emphasized the adolescent's resistance to analysis. "Since the child's immature ego is insecurely balanced between the pressures from within and without, he feels more threatened by analysis than the adult and his defenses are kept up more rigidly. This refers to the whole of childhood but is felt with special intensity at the beginning of adolescence" (Freud, 1965, 34). She adds later, "The adolescent needs to move away from his childhood objects, while analysis promotes the revival of the infantile relationships in the transference. This is felt as a special threat by the patient and frequently causes the abrupt ending of treatment" (Freud, 1965, 35).

At least Erikson suggested that adolescence not be viewed as an affliction but as a "normative crisis, i.e., a normal phase of increased conflict characterized by a seeming fluctuation in ego strength, and yet also by a high growth potential. What under prejudiced scrutiny may appear to be the onset of a neurosis, often is but an aggravated crisis which may be self-liquidating and, in fact, contribute to the process of identity formation" (1956). Nonetheless, the prevailing professional attitude has been jokingly conveyed by the statement, "Normal adolescence is a contradiction in terms."

In the Grinkers' (1962) classic paper on mentally healthy late adolescent males, they referred to their subjects as "Homoclites" and emphasized their lack of creativity and ambition and their boring personalities. The subjects were chosen because their test scores on the MMPI, a commonly used test of psychological functioning, were totally without pathology.

During the 1960s and 1970s, these views were subjected to objective scientific investigation of more inclusive samples of adolescents. Instead of generalizations based on clinical observations of troubled adolescents, Douvan and Adelson (1966) and later, Offer (1987), surveyed populations that included adolescents who had not been referred for therapy. The findings of these studies refuted many popular misconceptions regarding adolescence. The majority of youngsters in nonclinical samples reported themselves to be happy, confident, and free of the turbulence that had been attributed to the age group. Most of them also described positive relationships with their parents and other adults. Few of them were involved in rebellious behaviors; most did not even have rebellious attitudes. Only when Offer's group studied populations of emotionally disturbed and delinquent subgroups did they find the expected conflicts and problems. In the normal populations, only 20 percent of the adolescents mentioned serious adjustment problems. The attitude of mental health professionals had not changed, however. Seventy percent of a group of mental health workers scored *normal* adolescents as significantly more disturbed than *delinquent and disturbed* youth populations scored themselves (Offer, 1987). Even among professionals, the myth of adolescent unrest is slow to die. In summary, Offer and his associates described various successful paths through adolescence, only one of which featured the ballyhooed Sturm und Drang of popular clinical thinking.

In the past few years, two other images of the adolescent have been present in western cultural mythology. One expresses concern for those adolescents who are somewhat neglected due to the rising number of single-parent families and heightened work demands. Although this has been a pattern in the families of the working poor for some time, it is now recognized as common in the middle class as well. Patricia Hersh, in her book *A Tribe Apart* (1996), documents the pattern in a number of adolescents living in an affluent suburban area. She notes that most of the adolescents actually long for more supervision and support, despite the freedom they enjoyed.

The second image is a development that seems diametrically opposed to the sympathetic concern about relative neglect: our society's growing tendency to try adolescents who commit serious crimes as adults. In fact, these tendencies to demonize the serious delinquent and clamor for his punishment may be yet another facet of the adult disconnect from youth. This posture ignores the question of how the adolescent became so angry and destructive and washes society's collective hands of the responsibility to meet the developmental needs of our children and adolescents.

THE PSYCHOLOGICAL TASKS OF ADOLESCENCE
Adolescents seem to serve as a lightening rod, drawing a wide range of projections that may be more related to the prevailing

social currents than to the young people themselves. Most adolescents survive the period with reasonable comfort and without serious conflict with their environment. It is true that most of them report a fairly high level of anxiety, mainly related to external pressures most often associated with school. It may be that nervousness over the ever-changing and escalating demands of school might be more accurately called *fears*. In other words, the dangers are real, not imagined. In addition, no one who remembers the pressures of relating to rapidly changing peers is amazed to learn that socializing creates tension as well. Nevertheless, most adolescents juggle it all without dropping things too often.

However, most researchers of this developmental stage agree that the adolescent has to accomplish several psychological tasks in the years between childhood and adulthood. These adjustments may be accomplished without excessive emotional upset beyond the normal anxiety. This should not be taken as proof that the journey through adolescence is without peril and effort on the part of both parents and adolescents. The challenges of adolescence are probably equaled only by the adaptations necessary to aging and to becoming a parent. Like these two accommodations, adolescence involves major changes in self-image, personal responsibility, and one's relationship to the central people in one's life. The basic tasks of adolescence are demanding. Let's take a brief look at each of them:

1. The adolescent is expected to move toward greater independence and self-sufficiency. This requires relinquishing the dependent tie to the parents — at least to some extent. The younger adolescent often makes a show of fierce rebellion and distancing while simultaneously engaging in behaviors or verbalizations that ensure the parent will remain closely involved. With increasing maturity, the adolescent comes to understand that independence is best achieved by self-chosen interdependence with many people who can help one achieve goals — including parents.

2. The adolescent needs to restructure and to internalize his or her superego or conscience. The young child's moral sense is primarily based on parental wishes. Even intentionality is not considered. For example, if young children are asked if a child who accidentally breaks a valuable vase has done something worse than a child who deliberately smashes a cheap dish, they believe that the accidental damage is more culpable. Judgments of the young child also tend to be absolute — a behavior is either good or bad. The adolescent has to move beyond the assigned value system toward one that is chosen, which usually includes values similar to or identical to the parents, at least eventually. The creation of a self-developed, internal conscience leads to self-regulation of behavior based on avoiding feelings of guilt and shame by adhering to a personal moral standard. An adolescent stops worrying about getting caught with a hand in the cookie jar and begins to consider factors like the appetites of others, health issues, and the question of how one might feel later if gluttony prevails.

3. Another task, also closely tied to values, involves finding ways to adjust to the increases in sexual and aggressive impulses that accompany the biological changes of puberty. An adolescent girl can no longer regard sex as naughty if she is to incorporate her erotic urges in her personal identity. She certainly is that sort of girl — that is, one with sexual desires. The issues now involve how to express these urges. She must consider which circumstances and what timing is appropriate. The adolescent girl must consider her social standing and reputation as well as the risk of venereal disease, HIV, and pregnancy. The adolescent boy must decide how he feels about impregnating someone and his readiness to take responsibility for his sexual partner and perhaps for their child. Of course, the answers to these questions go beyond right and wrong and into practical issues of personal

responsibility for the possible consequences of sexual behavior. The adolescent doesn't want to be "bad," but even more the young person doesn't want to be "stupid." All these matters require not only decisions and plans but also the capacity to delay gratification and avoid situations where the stimulation and temptation might sweep away the best of intentions.

Aggression also takes on a new meaning during adolescence. Passive compliance — being nice — no longer solves most of life's issues. The complexities of middle school and high school culture press the adolescent to develop skills of self-assertion, defense of boundaries, comfortable competition, and even open conflict. No adolescent wants to be a wimp or a sucker. On the other hand, these priorities cannot be allowed to interfere with learning how to cooperate collegially with friends. If all this wasn't enough, the adolescent must learn how to be in a loving relationship with another person without being totally controlled or excessively domineering. There are many things to juggle.

4. As adolescents move forward in mastering these psychological tasks — to the extent that biological endowment and life experiences permit — they must also develop a sense of identity. Identity is based on personal characteristics such as similarities with and differences from parents and other influential adults, cultural and racial background, talents, moral beliefs, physical appearance, personal tastes and preferences, energy level, and a host of other defining variables. In addition, identity formation looks to the future, considering occupational interests and the likelihood of achieving those vocational goals. To serve its purpose effectively, the developing identity must reflect not only personal wishes and assessments of the self. It must at least approximate the possibilities for actualizing goals and aspirations in society using the skills that the adolescent either possesses or can develop with the level of sustainable effort that is within the

young person's capacity. This capacity may be affected by many factors. These include physical vigor and developed work habits but also include external factors such as encouragement or expectations coming from parents and other significant figures.

IS ADOLESCENCE A MORE
COMPLEX JOURNEY FOR ADOPTEES?

The overall adjustment of adopted adolescents is, in fact, good. The emotional health of adopted adolescents was found to be statistically better than a comparison group of adolescents from single parent families and comparable to the adjustment pattern of adolescents born into intact families (Brodzinsky, Smith, and Brodzinsky, 1998). There were only a few exceptions to this generalization:

- Adopted adolescents ran away from home more frequently than the control group adolescents.
- Adopted adolescents had a greater incidence of academic and school problems (Mathelin, 2004).
- Adopted adolescents were less likely to attend college.

As we discuss some of the special tasks faced by the adolescent adoptee, some of the reasons for the prevalence of these symptoms may become clearer. Although as stated, research points to a generally successful outcome for adopted adolescents and their families, clinical experience at C.A.S.E. suggests that this happy destination is achieved only after parents and adolescents go an extra mile. Adoption does complicate the necessary developmental progression through adolescence (Crook, 2000). Adoption should not be confused with psychopathology. Adoption is not something that is wrong. It is not a problem. However, it is a factual circumstance of great emotional importance. Like other givens that provide the backdrop for psychological development, it cannot be ignored. Let's discuss how some of the essential tasks of adolescence are especially complicated for the adopted young person.

The Adoptee and the Essential Tasks of Adolescence

Independence and Self-Sufficiency

The need to give up parental closeness in search of independence reawakens major loss issues for many adopted adolescents. Nydam (2000) says that many adopted children are "relinquishment sensitive," carrying the trauma of being "given up" throughout their lives. He further states that the primary effect regarding relinquishment during early childhood is anxiety; during latency it changes to sadness, and in adolescence it becomes anger. For transracial and transcultural adoptees, the early losses may also include loss of culture, loss of familiar language, and loss of surroundings.

In addition, to fill the void created by turning away from parents, adolescents turn to a peer group in which they can gain acceptance and support. If adopted adolescents, or their contemporaries, believe that adoption makes them different, then the comfort of the peer group may be compromised. The adopted adolescent may also find it awkward to complain about parents since that might sound ungrateful. Even if the adoptive parents have never asked for gratitude, the adolescent knows that society believes that gratitude is owed since the parents "rescued" the unwanted child. In addition, young people may also feel that they *should* feel appreciative. Therefore, this common bonding element for adolescent groups is less available to the adoptee. Adopted adolescents may feel very alone in their tentative move toward independence.

In some extreme cases, the adopted child has great trouble leaving home, even as a young adult. Many experts in the field say this common situation is related to an unspoken fear of total abandonment. Adopted people may believe, perhaps unconsciously, that the parents' responsibility is to pilot them to adulthood, and when that goal is accomplished, the parents' job is complete. This triggers the fear that they will lose yet another parent. Of course, with or without this terrifying notion, the other obstacles to emancipation apply.

Restructuring the Superego
The process of restructuring the superego is also complicated by adoption. The childish superego is based on a desire to please the parents and to follow their rules, as discussed earlier. Of course, these desires focus on pleasing an idealized and near-perfect parent. During adolescence youngsters not only see the imperfections in the parent, they exaggerate the faults. This is not only painful for the parent, but it also leaves a vacuum for the adolescent, a space that is often filled by crushes and idealizations focused on celebrities or idealized individuals outside of the family. For some adopted adolescents there is the risk of idealizing the birth parents — who may not be known — thereby blocking the process of creating their own value system.

Adjusting to Increased Sexual Urges and Aggression
The normal upsurge of aggressive and sexual urges in the adolescent, coupled with the need to restructure the conscience, may interfere with identification with the adoptive parents. If the adopted youngster believes (rightly or wrongly) that the birth parents were poor or antisocial, the young person may take the intensified drives as evidence that he or she is genetically inferior to the adoptive parents and must be just like the birth parents. As a result, the adoptee may embrace hedonism and rebellion toward the "square and restrictive" adoptive parents or wallow in a guilty sense of unworthiness. Usually these attitudes oscillate, creating a pattern of acting out followed by periods of remorse and self-recrimination. Conversely, the adoptive parents may be secretly afraid that the teen will end up like the birth parents, unintentionally projecting this fear onto the child and creating a self-fulfilling prophecy.

CASE EXAMPLE

Rosa, a thirteen-year-old Hispanic girl born in South America, is referred for therapy by her Caucasian North American parents. They are deeply concerned because Rosa has become angry, rebellious, and verbally abusive at home. This behavior is in marked contrast to the behaviors and attitudes that she had demonstrated in the years since she was brought from an orphanage in very early childhood. In addition, the parents have overheard suspicious telephone conversations that suggest that Rosa is involved in secret liaisons with boys.

Interestingly, Rosa makes no objections to being interviewed by a therapist. In fact, she speaks openly of her sense that her family is "too good" for her. She soon confesses that she is sexually active with two different Hispanic boys that she had met at the mall. She feels somewhat guilty about her behavior but she is also very proud of her newfound popularity. She is also frightened that she might be pregnant and is terrified of the prospect of telling her parents. "They will probably send me back. They should." When the therapist suggested that her obnoxious behavior toward the parents might be an effort to encourage them to reject her, she wept and agreed. She decided that she wanted to confess to her parents and did so. The parents noted an immediate reduction in her hostile behavior at home. However, Rosa still needed months of psychotherapy to become comfortable with her sexuality. She assumed her birth mother was promiscuous and that her sexual urges were her Hispanic heritage. Her parents, who were actually quite liberal and understanding, were of enormous help in Rosa's effort to understand that sexuality was a positive element of life — not a dirty secret that made her unworthy of their love.

● ●

The Search for Identity

The normal adolescent search for identity also has many complicating elements for the adopted adolescent. To be sure, the task of integrating a personal sense of identity is difficult for all adolescents. The process includes self-evaluation and interaction with one's personal world. Perhaps more importantly, the task involves accepting and incorporating the positive personality and cognitive contributions of parents while asserting differences from them. This process is obviously even more confusing for adopted adolescents. These young people must factor in the heritage of the birth family in addition to working out their heritage from the adoptive parents. The presence of two connections to early childhood — one biological and historical, the other parental and present — may make it difficult for the adolescent to totally emancipate from either. The normal regressive pulls created by the sometimes fearful prospect of independence may draw the adolescent first to one dependent tie and then to the other, confusing the effort to establish identity.

Intense fantasies regarding birth parents, which adoptees with closed adoptions often have, may distort the effort to establish a rational and usable self-image. For example, if the adolescent imagines that the birth parents would be more nurturing, permissive, and hedonistic than the adoptive parents, that can lead to rejection of the positive expectations with which the youngster has been reared. Conversely, the adolescent may reject the birth parents if they are believed to be immoral and despicable. Unfortunately, this may also secretly corrode the adolescent's sense of his or her own goodness and strength. Such a youth may view him- or herself as a weak and unworthy person, saved by powerful and godlike adoptive parents. Many adopted youngsters say that their fantasies about birth parents tend to swing between extremes of idealization and derision.

The path for adoptive parents is treacherous, too. They may find the process of normal emancipation with its exaggerated poses of rejection of parents and parental values difficult to tolerate. The parents may see this posturing — which may actually be exaggerated when adolescents are insecure — as evidence of a total disruption of the relationship with their child. This is especially likely if one or both of the parents go into the adolescent period with doubts about their child's acceptance of them as being his "true parents," or with self doubts about their role as "true parents."

Parents who have not come to peace with their emotional reaction to infertility are particularly vulnerable. The typical criticism of the parent — "you're not my mother, I don't have to listen to you" — may trigger feelings of inferiority and deficiency related to the adoptive parents' conflicts around their inability to conceive. How stinging, then, are comments that start like this: "My *real* mother wouldn't..." As one teen shouted to his mom, "If God had meant for you to be a mother, he would have let you have a baby." In a related way, adoptive parents may reject their children with the fantasy that their biological children would have been more compatible.

Persisting feelings of shame or guilt undermine the secure self-confidence parents need in order to maintain equanimity amidst sometimes turbulent and rapidly changing emotions of the adolescent. One parent, speaking of her adolescent's rejection of her, exclaimed, "What I am suffering from is unrequited love!" How much more difficult to tolerate this perceived betrayal if one has never been fully confident of the child's love or in the parental role. The situation may be further compounded by the adolescent's increased interest in the birth parents. "Not only is my child rejecting my parenting, he seems to prefer other people who have done little or nothing for him." This embattled adoptive family must tolerate and even support the adolescent's wish to search for the birth parents.

This often fans the fear that the adolescent will prefer the other family and reject the adoptive parents. In any case, the adoptive parents often are required to accept the birth parents in fantasy or in the flesh and to facilitate their inclusion in the psychological inner circle of the adolescent. This can be very difficult if the birth parents' socioeconomic or moral background is drastically at variance with those of the adoptive parents.

Considering the bewildering complexities the adopted adolescent faces in negotiating the winding paths of adolescence, it is a small wonder that many of them require the services of a trained guide. That would be us — therapists who offer treatment to adolescents. However, if we are to be reliable pilots, we need to take a moment to look at the ways adoption may affect our attitudes and also the ways the adoptee may experience our efforts to help.

Every time I brought up my adoption with therapists, they said,
"I am sure you and your family feel very lucky to have one another."
It was so hard for me to speak about my anger, confusion, and
sometimes overwhelming sense of sadness about being adopted.
Julia

CHAPTER 2

self-analysis

the therapist's attitude toward

the adopted adolescent

In the treatment approach that we call psychotherapy, the only tool we have is ourselves. Most of us work hard to calibrate this instrument through study, supervision, therapy, and introspection. It is important that we do this with regard to special tasks that may confront us in the treatment of the adopted adolescent.

The Dave Thomas Foundation for Adoption, in cooperation with the Evan B. Donaldson Adoption Institute, undertook a national adoption attitudes survey. The results were published in June 2002 and may be of value to us as we review our own personal attitudes toward adoption.

The survey results are interesting. Sixty-three percent of the survey population had a favorable view of adoption. Of course, that means that a third of the population did not. Eighty-two percent said that, should they adopt, they would worry that the birth parents would change their minds and try to get the child back. This finding is probably the result of the sensational media coverage given to the rare instances when this does occur. There are many other interesting findings. For example, adults who adopt infants and very young children are perceived to be motivated by the desire to form a family. On the other hand, people who adopt older children and children in foster care are assumed to have the altruistic goal of providing a good home for the child!

A study is currently under way surveying therapists with similar questionnaires to determine attitudes of this group. Unfortunately, no results are available yet. Therefore, we can only recommend that therapists perform their own self-searching to recognize any biases and preconceived negative attitudes they may harbor regarding adoption. If a friend or family member has had a negative experience with adoption, the individual therapist may overgeneralize and assume that these experiences are more common than, in fact, they are.

The nature of the adoptive event itself creates some potential problems. We can only help by highlighting some of the common counter-transference traps that may be particularly dangerous in the treatment of the adopted adolescent. All of them can be difficult to avoid in treating any adolescent, but they are especially powerful forces in adopted youngsters.

REJECTION OF THE DEPENDENT RELATIONSHIP TO THE THERAPIST

All adolescents are wary of depending on a therapist. Because of the healthy regression in the service of growth that occurs normally during this developmental period, the adolescent is beset by strong dependency yearnings that must be actively spurned and denied. Bombastic demands for freedom to live their lives without adult direction are common. Belittlement and derision are generously offered to the adults who dare to offer advice! Obviously, therapists are special threats since, by definition, their role is to minister to young people who are troubled and in need have helped.

Adolescents who actually need help are especially likely to see all dependency as childlike and demeaning. They often lack the self-confidence to understand and believe that dependency can be voluntarily chosen to gain assistance in a particular area. They are blind to the fact that this choice can actually enhance functioning, strengthen competence, and foster successful independence. Consequently, many troubled adolescents fear therapy and are not comforted by the therapist's empathy and warmth. Paradoxically, they may be threatened by their own positive response to the caring adult, fearing that they will become too dependent. There is not only the shame of wishing for the childlike relationship; there is also the anticipation of potential rejection when the therapist discovers their guilty secret failings.

Can you imagine how much more painful these conflicts are for adopted children? They have already been discarded by one set of parents and are nervously trying to emancipate without losing their second set. They often harbor notions that they have terrible faults that led their birth parents to reject them. They often feel guilty about their ambivalence toward their adoptive parents. They think that they have a lot to hide.

The result for the therapist is often a powerful attack on one's identity as a helpful adult. The adopted adolescent often rejects the entire therapeutic endeavor — in fact, often negates the need for, and the very possibility of, therapeutic benefit. Rosa, the adopted youngster described in chapter 1, faked sleep throughout her first evaluation session. In his article, Frank Salamone (2000) describes how he was unable to face his intense, hidden feelings about his adoption until his *fifth* therapist gently but firmly broke down his resistance.

Even if the adopted adolescent acknowledges the need for treatment, resistence may surface around the effort to explore the adoption issues. We have described the powerful forces that lead the adopted adolescent to avoid the emotional issues involved in the adoption experience. Because of these, the therapist encounters reactions ranging from bland denial to angry avoidance. At the same time, the therapy is doomed to fail if the therapist is not successful in the effort to open this area of inquiry. The frustration of this paradox can easily lead to irritation and wishes to blame and even reject the adopted patient. Most of us do not enjoy feeling helpless and are rarely grateful to those who arouse those feelings in us. A strong sense of personal worth and professional confidence is vital to the therapist's patience and willingness to creatively search for the proper technique for the individual adolescent. One size definitely does *not* fit all, and it can be very trying to discover the comfortable style for the grumpy adopted adolescent.

● ●

CASE EXAMPLE

Amy was adopted as an infant. She formed a close attachment to her adoptive parents. The parents adopted a boy two years later. Amy doted on her new brother and was described as a "sunny and very happy" preschool youngster. However, when she started school it soon became apparent that she had severe learning problems. Still, with the strong support of her parents, she persevered and eventually made it through college. She became very dependent on her parents during her academic trials and had some struggle in emancipating. That struggle led to a period of psychotherapy as a young adult. She made some progress although she steadfastly denied any problems regarding her adoption and said she had no interest in information about her birth parents. After a time she was able to emancipate, fall in love, and marry. She was considering ending therapy but she became pregnant unexpectedly and decided to stay on for a while. When she

Beneath the Mask

announced the pregnancy to the therapist, the therapist commented, "It must be really exciting to look forward to having a blood relative." Amy replied, "My mother is really thrilled about it." The therapist was able gently to connect Amy's comment with her difficulty in looking honestly at her feelings about her origins. She gradually realized that she had given all she had to her adopted mother — including her inner feelings.

● ●

THE OMNIPOTENCE OF ADOLESCENT THOUGHT

The process of psychotherapy requires objective self-observation, honest recognition of personal strengths and weaknesses, and, finally, testing ideas and plans against external reality. There are several developmental reasons why these tasks do not come naturally to many adolescents. During the adolescent period, there is a natural increase in omnipotent thinking. Like most developmental changes, this habit of thought has eventual adaptive value. Since adolescents must cope with a growing recognition of the mounting pressures that will be faced in adulthood, they need to think expansively and positively of their abilities.

During the same period, cognitive development is progressing toward comfortable manipulation of abstraction — the phase of cognition that Piaget called Formal Operations. This allows the adolescent to think about hypothetical possible futures and about the reason behind events. The overall effect is that the adolescent has a powerful computer but rather limited data to input, to use an analogy from technology. Therefore, the adolescent places an excessive value on thought as compared with experience. Solutions to society's major problems are obvious and adult failure to implement them clearly demonstrates the incompetence or malevolence of the grownup world. The intelligent adolescent often spends a significant

self-analysis   21 amount of therapy time lecturing and educating the therapist. Frequently, they are exasperated with the dim-witted responses of their adult student.

Many adopted adolescents show these traits in exaggerated form. Therefore, from still another quarter, the therapist's narcissism is under assault. The temptation to offer sage advice, sensible warnings, and even sarcastic comments can be strong. Of course, any of these responses will strengthen the adolescent's resistance to adult intervention. The therapist is experienced as controlling, condescending, and disrespectful of the adolescent's fledgling efforts to come to grips with the adult world. What the adolescent needs is recognition and praise of his intelligent thought coupled with only cautious efforts to input information in the form of polite and respectful questions.

Tony, a bright adopted fourteen-year-old, was furious at all adults. He railed against his teachers, his parents, and the laws of the land. Tony derided all legislation based on age; for example, the need to be seventeen in order to get a driver's license. This and all laws like it were obvious examples of the inept grown-ups robbing talented young people of their rights.

Fortunately, Tony also skewered his peers, particularly when he felt they were acting immaturely. This allowed the therapist to ask if Tony thought those youngsters should be licensed to drive. The point was to discuss the variability in the rate of maturation and to ask Tony if he could come up with a more fair system of deciding who could operate an automobile safely. The goal of the therapist was to help Tony expand his intelligence to include more facts and a wider focus.

Remember that adopted adolescents have special reasons to feel the adult world has failed. Birth parents abandoned them and now they must deal with accepting the human imperfections of their adoptive parents that they may be reluctant to openly acknowledge. It is much safer and less emotionally loaded to attack adults in general and often the therapist in particular.

The adolescent propensity to idealism is a related element of this therapeutic complication. Most adolescents have heroines and heroes, complete with glittering haloes provided by idealization. Sometimes these are celebrities; sometimes they are people that the adolescent actually knows personally. These icons serve as stand-ins for the previously idealized parents who must now be dethroned in the process of emancipation. The idols also represent projected qualities that the adolescent aspires toward or at least wishes to achieve. In the case of admired peers or slightly older acquaintances, the admiration is sometimes mutual, as both parties see strengths in the other and gain self-esteem through the shared acceptance. All of these psychological events serve the purpose of aiding the development of identity and the maturing of the conscience.

The adopted adolescent may have special need of these maturational techniques. The complexity of the dual family constellation may make seeking external role models particularly appealing. It may be very hard for the merely mortal therapist to measure up to these paragons of whatever the adolescent seeks — honesty, virtue, courage, beauty, strength — the list is endless. The situation may be particularly difficult in those cases in which the adolescent chooses the unknown birth parent as the ultimate perfection. The therapist then is not only colorless and uninteresting but actually another obstacle preventing the sublime happiness that could easily occur if only the young person could be reunited with the idealized parent.

The temptation to puncture this obviously unrealistic bubble is strong. It is also tempting to identify with the beleaguered adoptive parents who are getting the same treatment as you are. The therapist may also experience considerable anxiety and a strong need to "do something" due to the fear that the adopted adolescent may run away or engage in other dangerous efforts to rejoin the birth parent or parents. The adolescent's fervent belief that all problems would disappear with reunion often appears so misguided as to almost seem psychotic. Indeed it is alarming. Furthermore, the adoptive parents may be putting extreme pressure on the therapist to "talk some sense into the child."

The therapist often has the uncomfortable role of gradually helping both parties to accept that immediate action is not the solution. The parents often respond to education regarding the developmental sources of the adolescent's fantasy and the likelihood that further therapy and maturation will resolve the problem. (We discuss birth parent preoccupation and search wishes in more detail in chapters that follow.)

Managing the situation with the adolescent can be more trying, especially in the face of derision and dismissal of the therapist's comments and opinions. In some cases, adolescents do provide an opening by trying to elicit the therapist's help in convincing the adoptive parents to let them go to their birth parent. Even the adamant adolescent can grudgingly accept the therapist's position that support would not be possible without much more information. The therapist can tell the youngster, " I understand that you are totally convinced this is the right thing to do. Perhaps it is, but I would not be able to say that without a lot more knowledge of the whole situation. Even though you are in a big hurry, I need some time and a lot of data to back up such an important decision." The therapist should, however, make it clear that adopted youngsters' right to know the facts about their origins may need to be delayed but never denied.

This position also creates a contract that even allows the therapist to raise questions about the adolescent's certainty. One can say, "Hold on just a minute. You're telling me you have never met your birth mother? How are you so sure she is ready to be a parent?" Alternatively, "Let me get this straight. Your birth mother had to give you up because she was using drugs, but things are much better now? Tell me what you know about the present situation. How did you learn about the improvement? How long has she been off drugs?" After a bit, the therapist may even gently challenge the adolescent. "So your mom has been clean three months. I've been told that chemical dependency therapists say people who have quit shouldn't make any major life changes for at least a year. Are you at all worried that it might not be good for your mom to take over all this responsibility so soon?"

Of course, the adolescent will be happy to set you straight. "Of course it would be good for her. I want to be there to help her."

The therapist has to be quick. "Well, of course I know that. I was just thinking that she might worry about your school problems or other stuff that goes on with young adults. You do have your own life."

As a matter of fact, dealing with any impulsive or poorly conceived plan with *any* adolescent is a somewhat risky business. It is very important to avoid authoritarian stances and to "say no the ego way" (Meeks and Bernet, 2001). This approach appeals not to power but to the adolescent's good judgment. No matter how careful the therapist is, the adolescent may still see any delay or questioning as a forbidden parental intrusion into autonomy. One can only monitor one's motivations and edit one's therapeutic behavior to ensure against actually slipping into adult bossy control. If one's therapeutic heart is pure, it is easier to deflect and defuse adolescent criticism without being defensive.

THE THERAPIST AS REAL OBJECT
One unavoidable fact in treating adolescents is that in this developmental period the young person is still seeking and using real objects, that is, adults, to emulate, learn from, and eventually to internalize as part of the psyche. If the adolescent is able to form a trusting therapeutic relationship with the therapist, that adult will also play this role to some extent.

Of course, early in therapy the adolescent will have many attitudes and images regarding the therapist that are a product of the transference. Unfortunately, the adolescent often has great difficulty in separating transference fantasies from reality. Often it is as though the adolescent is thinking, "What I see is what you are."

Every experienced adolescent therapist can recount numerous, sometimes amusing, examples of mistaken assumptions that adolescent patients have harbored regarding the therapist's personality or interests. These fanciful ideas may be based on past experiences the adolescent has had with significant adults or on personal wishes or fears. Much of the work of therapy consists of recognizing the clues and hints of such distortions and devising therapeutically constructive ways to help the adolescent to see one more accurately and thus to learn more about themselves.

In the case of the adopted adolescent, this task is sometimes more complex. The adoptive experience does not provide the simple anchor of established, uncontestable parenthood. Granted, even nonadopted adolescents may fantasize that the therapist is actually the perfect parent they have always desired, but even to them, that is clearly imaginary. In the case of the adopted adolescent, who is to say for sure that it isn't true? In any case, certainly the therapist could conceivably adopt the patient. Younger adopted children, especially those from foster care, often ask the therapist to take them home and parent them. Adolescents are too proud to say so as a rule, but that doesn't mean they don't think about it. Since it is obvious that these young people do not need another parental rejection, handling these wishes without embarrassing or hurting them can be a delicate matter (Tubero, 2002).

Conversely, one must take care to avoid promising in word or in deed what cannot be delivered. Most therapists do not make verbal promises. However, subtle failures to observe appropriate therapeutic boundaries may speak very loudly to the young person. Often these errors are motivated by genuine empathy for the adolescent and by positive regard and affection. Buying gifts, doing favors, or providing contact outside of the therapeutic context may convince the young person that the therapist is committed to taking real, parentlike responsibility for them. The result may be an escalation of behaviors unconsciously designed to elicit the therapist's concern and greater

Beneath the Mask

personal involvement. It is probably true that self-revelation, to a limited and appropriate extent, is more common and even valuable in treating adoptive families. Many of the professionals in the field are themselves adopted or are adoptive parents — sometimes both. Sharing this fact often makes it easier for families and adolescents to believe that the therapist has some familiarity with the special problems in the adoptive family. However, these professionals recognize the privacy rights of others in their families and do not divulge information about them. For example, the adoptive parent therapist would not share his or her child's adoption story with a client.

The experience of treating adolescents is designed to keep therapists nimble and humble. In young people's powerful reach toward a true understanding of adulthood that is compatible with their unique character and personality, they will test those who dare to become involved with them. Initially, the test relates to the safety of the encounter. The adolescent checks out the adult to be sure that the grown-up is not stupid, weak, judgmental, arrogant, or controlling. If the therapist understands the questions — which are rarely posed directly — and comes up with suitable answers, the adolescent proceeds to conduct the second page of the exam. In that section, the therapist is examined as a human being. The adolescent wants to know how this grown-up handles the problems in his or her life that are like those that confront the young person. Is it possible for the therapist to accept criticism without getting mad and without undue self-blame? Is it possible to be accepting of sexuality without being drawn into supporting inappropriate sex?

Can one be angry without being destructive? How can one succeed even if one is not free of faults and weaknesses? This list of queries is never posed directly, goes on and on, and varies from youngster to youngster. Adolescents use arguing, hypothetical queries, discussions of third parties, and many other gambits to gain the information they want to get without embarrassing themselves. For example, the adolescent may describe a friend who is shrewd enough to get away with negative or even illegal actions. The young client may profess admiration for this wily character in order to discuss the proper basis of ethical behavior. If the therapist is not moralistic and expresses concern and sympathy for youngsters who step outside the rules while clearly stating a personal belief that there are more productive and fair approaches to life, the young person gains support for mature conscience development. The therapist needs to be alert to these indirect queries and understand and respond to each one.

The questions of the adopted adolescent are not different from the questions of the nonadopted adolescent, but they may be more complex and convoluted because of the additional people involved and the unique experience of each adopted youngster. This complexity may sometimes tax the therapist's understanding, but empathy and comfortable self-scrutiny often guide one to a successful conclusion.

As an adoptive parent I had never thought about what it would be like to be adopted. I had read all the books but before this assessment no one had ever posed the question to me in that way.
Clara, adoptive Mom

CHAPTER 3

The C.A.S.E. Assessment Model

Assessing the Adopted Adolescent

Despite the historical perspective that adoption adjustment is complex and that the experience of adoption creates certain vulnerabilities that may predispose adopted teens to require therapeutic interventions, it is often difficult to gain access to these issues with adolescent adoptees in therapy. The challenge for many therapists in assessing adoption issues in therapy can be manifested in varying situations, as noted by Zuckerman and Buschsbaum (2000).

Initially the parents may minimize the emotional importance of the "event" of adoption. There can be many reasons for this denial. The parents themselves may be struggling with unresolved losses associated with infertility. In other cases, the child's initial symptomatolgy is so dramatic that the focus is diverted from exploring adoption-related issues. Talking about adoption may also not be a comfortable process for a teen and their family. Early adoption practice promoted secrecy in adoption. Although much progress has been made in openness about adoption, many parents still fear that talking about adoption will stir things up, causing kids to think about things that they would not have brought up on their own. A very good reason to keep adoption out of the therapy office!

Clinicians evaluating the adopted adolescent will need to open the door for exploration of the myriad of adoption-related issues affecting the adolescent. In many clinical practices, adoption issues are not addressed in the assessment. At best, the question of adoption status may simply be posed: Are you adopted? We explore in later chapters some of the reasons why therapists may not be comfortable with adoption as it relates to their personal beliefs and awareness about adoption. However, an overriding myth that adoption created a "happy" solution to the problems of everyone involved has been rigorously challenged over the past thirty-five years. Although adoption was, and remains, a viable solution to infertility as well as an option for birth parents who for a variety of reasons choose not to parent their children, adoption by no means is without complexities and problems. Problems may persist for all those woven into the adoption tapestry — birth parents, adoptive parents, and the children. To be competent adoption specialists, therapists must recognize that the impact of adoption is lifelong; it is not something that is eventually forgotten. In fact, the impact is intricately woven in the fabric of every adoptee's life (Brodzinsky, Schechter, and Henig, 1993).

For the therapist, the first step in affirming adoption is demonstrating their own comfort level in discussing the topic of adoption and the potential questions and feelings adoption will raise in the assessment process. The more therapists work with adopted teens, the more familiar they will become with the complex issues surrounding adoption and the approach they will take in joining with the adolescent around adoption. The goal is for the adolescent to truly believe the therapist's competency as an adoption specialist. We all know how untrusting adolescents are in general and the low regard they have for yet another adult who knows more than they do! Brace yourself for their ability to minimize your effectiveness and their denial that adoption has anything to do with why they may be sitting in your office.

During the initial interview, it is essential that adoption be affirmed and that the adolescent senses the therapist's comfort in speaking about adoption. When the therapist embraces the adoption experience, it can have the immediate positive therapeutic effect of lowering the shame and secrecy embedded in the adolescent's mind. Too often, teens reported that they saw many therapists who never asked them about their adoption. Worse, they may have the experience that Julia described with great sadness: "Every time I brought up my adoption, they said, 'I am sure you and your family feel very lucky to have one another.' It was so hard for me to speak about my anger; confusion and sometimes-overwhelming sense of sadness about being adopted." Julia, age fourteen, was referred by her school counselor after writing a suicide note to her best friend in class. Adoption played a significant role in Julia's depression. However, the parents reported several evaluators did not explore adoption issues with Julia and/or them before they came to C.A.S.E.

●●●●●●●●●●●●●●●●●●●●●●●●

CASE EXAMPLE

Matthew entered therapy at age thirteen after running away from home for an extended period of time. He was referred by his school principal, who became involved in this crisis when Matthew refused to return home after school one day. Matthew told the principal that he wanted his parents out of his life. Following several conversations with his parents, they agreed to meet with the therapist without their son to provide a thorough history. During the assessment, they revealed Matthew was adopted at five months of age and had very little adoption history to share. They were surprised at their son's departure and very much wanted him to return home.

Matthew continued to refuse to return home, staying with the family of a close peer but did agree to come to therapy without his parents. Matthew's parents gave permission for the therapist to see him separately. Initially Matthew, like most adolescents, engaged in much posturing and bravado. He felt he could take care of himself and certainly he did not need his "older" parents to guide him through life. In fact they were so old that they were out of touch with his world and what was important to him. After allowing Matthew to vent his omnipotence, the therapist asked Matthew why he was placed for adoption. Quiet and pensive now, Matthew thought long and hard and then answered with flowing tears, "I guess I cried too much when I was a baby." So much for taking bravado at face value! Matthew reminded us again of the power of relinquishment and the untouched feelings associated with it. Respectful, gentle probing along with helping the teen to make a connection to adoption is the beginning of the therapeutic alliance.

● ● ● ● ● ● ● ● ● ● ● ● ● ● ● ● ● ● ● ●

C.A.S.E. ASSESSMENT MODEL

Empirical and anecdotal information indicates that "adoption competent mental health services are lacking for post-finalized adoptive families" (Smith and Howard, 1999). The significance of adoption-related issues largely are ignored or minimized by clinicians, who focus therapeutically on the myriad of externalizing behaviors teens often present. The techniques and approaches outlined here originated and have been refined at C.A.S.E. as we strive to address the inherent complexities of the adoption experience for adolescents.

C.A.S.E.'s assessment model is built upon several key tenets that guide the assessment and therapeutic process. More important than a clinician's theoretical framework and specific treatment approach is a thorough understanding of adoption related issues and when and how they may surface within the therapeutic process. Many of the following tenets are explored in more depth in chapter 4.

1. Adoption is a circumstance of emotional importance that affects all members of the adoption circle.

2. Adoption is not pathological. There are predictable developmental stages that vary from child to child, but all adoptees will move through each differently and each with different impact (Pavao, 1998).

3. Adoptive families and their children face unique challenges inherent in adoption and different from forming a family by birth (Kirk, 1964).

4. Adoption is a lifelong process (Brodzinsky et al., 1993).

5. Adoptive loss is unique and pervasive in all adoption adjustment. It is ambiguous and often misunderstood (Boss, 1999).

6. Individuals bring personality, resiliency, temperament, and strengths to the adoption experience; no two adoptive experiences are the same.

7. Six tasks inherent to adoption can create emotional stressors for members of the adoptive family: reason for adoption, missing

or difficult information, difference, permanence, identity, and loyalty. (These are addressed in detail in chapter 4.)

8. Adoption-related issues must be treated in a family system context (Reitz and Watson, 1992).

9. Information empowers the adoptee and reduces uncertainty.

10. Children do think about their birth families frequently and intently.

11. Children need help in integrating their history prior to adoption. They should not be asked to forget.

12. Environmental, relational, and organic stresses of preadoptive (and prenatal) experiences can significantly impact physical and brain development, adjustment, and attachment.

13. Adolescent adoptees have two sets of parents to separate from.

14. Talking about adoption is positive and promotes healthy adjustment.

Mental health professionals must understand these issues unique to adoption. Key to this insight is an awareness of how it truly feels to be adopted and how the teen's life is affected by being adopted both intrapersonally and interpersonally. Remember, this is not an intellectual exercise; this is a highly emotional event.

The assessment needs to be thorough, taking into consideration the complexities of adoption through a developmental lens. In addition to this understanding of adoption issues, the therapist must have a strong clinical foundation with emphasis on adolescent development and family systems theory. Exploring the experience of adoption with both the parents and the adolescent at this time is an integral part of the assessment interview.

Typically, when conducting the assessment for an adolescent, the therapist will meet first with the parents and teen to explain the process and clarify what brought the family to seek services. Very often the therapist will obtain general information, family composition, the teen's academic status, peer/family relations, and explore the teen's adoption story with both parents and teen present. Following this, the parents are seen separately for a period of time and then the therapist meets with the adolescent individually. The assessment concludes with all parties rejoining for closure and recommendations. Let's examine the steps in the C.A.S.E. assessment model.

ASSESSMENT OF ADOPTIVE PARENTS

The assessment begins with the reasons surrounding the parents' decision to build a family through adoption. The preadoptive experiences of the adoptive parents play a significant role in determining the later functioning of the adoptive family unit. Special attention should be given to both partners' perceptions as to why they chose adoption and the circumstances that led to the adoption decision. For example, the therapist will want to explore whether the adoption was a result of infertility, single parenthood, or same-sex relationship.

If the couple experienced infertility, the therapist needs to explore many issues. Was the couple able to master the loss and grief issues related to their inability to conceive before they decided to adopt? Were both partners diagnosed with infertility issues or just one of them? What is the couple's eventual acceptance of their infertility? Although infertility issues may never be totally resolved, the couple needs to incorporate the loss into a healthy, functioning sense of self. The first step is to recognize and acknowledge the loss connected to their infertility (Brodzinsky et al., 1998). This acknowledgment is followed by varying degrees of grief, guilt, shame, and gradual growth and compensation. Inadequate resolution of infertility conflicts can negatively affect the adoptive parents' relationship with their child. For many parents, these issues are reawakened and intensified in adolescence, when the teen's sexuality is heightening and the youngster's fertility is evident. In some cases it may play a role in early pregnancy in adopted adolescent girls. If the parent is a single adoptive parent, questions should focus upon how this person came to adoption as a way to build a family, what external support systems the person has in place, and whether there is a significant other who will be involved in the parenting.

Adoption History

The therapist will also want to take a thorough adoption history. Several important questions need to be explored. At what age was the child placed? If the child was not placed at birth, where did the child live prior to joining the family? with a foster family? in an orphanage? with relatives or other caregivers? How long did the child remain in their care? Were there multiple caregivers? What was the child's relationship with previous caregivers? Did the adoption placement disrupt important attachments? Were there any indications of abuse and/or neglect in previous care-giving situations? Were there siblings from whom the child was separated? Were they reunited? If the siblings were adopted into another home, where are they now? What relationship do they have at this time?

As central to all developmental histories, the clinician will also want to delve into pre- and postnatal information. Parents are asked to share what information they have, if any, regarding their knowledge of prenatal care, the pregnancy, delivery, and birth family's medical and social history, as well as the child's developmental milestones. A detailed and dependable developmental history may or may not be available in cases of adoption. We encourage therapists to ask parents to share what they do know and not to judge them as irresponsible if they do not have a comprehensive pool of information. It is important to understand that the parents have control only over what information was given to them during the placement process. If the child was adopted at birth, the adoptive parents generally can articulate information regarding developmental milestones, speech and language development, growth patterns, cognitive abilities, and temperamental characteristics. For later-placed children, many of these facts may be unavailable. This may limit diagnostic and therapeutic planning, but it is often an unavoidable deficit in treating adopted teens. Clinicians must do the best they can given the fact that this potentially valuable information may be sketchy or absent. Remember too that adolescents may be sensitive to these questions surrounding their histories. Teens often exhibit fears and anxieties when health issues, which may have a genetic basis, emerge. Often they carry concerns that some terrible illness may be lurking in their shadowy genetic past.

Of all the predictors of positive adoption adjustment, age of placement is the most critical factor. Research demonstrates that the older a child is at placement, the greater the risk for the placement to end in dissolution (Brodzinsky, 1998; Howard and Smith, 1999). Furthermore, children placed from the public child welfare system and/or those who have been in orphanage care are also at risk for developing adoption adjustment problems as they mature. If the therapist makes a careful review of the teen's exposure to multiple caregivers, institutionalization, neglect, and/or abuse prior to placement in the adoptive family, then the therapist can help the teen and the adoptive parents understand the entire picture.

We have learned at C.A.S.E. that obtaining a thorough preplacement history is essential when treating a later-placed teen. Often, families will communicate that they were given conflicted information or no information at all by adults involved in the placement process, whether it was a domestic or international adoption. This leaves everyone to operate in the dark. Striking elements in the adolescent's clinical picture may sometimes offer clues.

● ●

CASE EXAMPLE

Valerie was adopted from an eastern European orphanage at age six. She made an excellent adjustment to her new home and new country. She was bright and affectionate, learning the new language and enthusiastically accepting all things American. She made friends easily, had many interests, did well in school, and chattered to her parents, trustfully sharing her every thought.

Then adolescence struck.

Although her positive adjustment continued, she became quieter and more secretive. All was well until an evening when her mother went out to play bridge, leaving Valerie at home with her father. Her father was watching a television program he felt Valerie would enjoy and called her over. Valerie came a little reluctantly as she was on the computer and didn't want to be bothered by a stupid show her father was watching. She entered the family room and testily asked, "What?" He playfully grabbed her and pulled her down on his lap, as he had done many times before. He was astonished when Valerie screamed and leapt off the couch. "What do you think you're doing?" she screeched at him and ran away to her room. When he followed her and knocked on the door, she tearfully told him to go away.

Over the next few weeks Valerie's rejection of her father intensified. She seemed to loathe him and shrank from his touch. She told her mother that she was afraid of him. "I don't know what he's going to do," she confided.

The parents brought Valerie back to the therapist who had counseled them around adoption issues years before. After an evaluation, the therapist suspected that Valerie might have been molested at the orphanage. The concern that abuse may have occurred in the past was communicated to the parents, and it was recommended that Valerie engage in therapy.

● ●

Communication around Adoption

Based on our experiences at C.A.S.E, we have coined a mantra: "Talking Is Good for Everyone." However, we know that not all families operate on this premise. The therapist will want to explore the family's comfort level with talking about adoption. Does the family embrace a belief system opposed to discussing adoption? Is secrecy a family dogma? If the parents do believe that communication around adoption is okay, where do they fall along the continuum of openness? How was the child's adoption status presented? At what age? Who delivered the information — mother, father, or both together? Was the full content of the story presented to the child? How did the parents present the reasons for relinquishment by the birth parents? What was the child's reaction? Were the parents able to handle the child's reaction to adoption? Did they support the expression of feelings and validate their justification?

Too often adoptive parents try to alleviate the painful feelings held by their children. Unfortunately, this sometimes squelches the youngster's expression. Therapists should be on the lookout for this and help parents to see that their children will have varying feelings regarding their adoption and often need the parents to just be accepting of them: to just sit with the youngster and share the feelings. This can be very painful and sad for the parent.

Focusing on the adolescent's experience may lead to further questions. For example, what, if any, aspects of the adoption experience have not yet been shared with the young person? Frequently parents will reveal that they are holding on to information that they find difficult to share because they believe it will have negative implications for their teen.

●　●　●　●　●　●　●　●　●　●　●　●　●　●　●　●　●　●　●

CASE EXAMPLE

John and Amanda were concerned about Patrick, their seventeen-year-old son, now a senior in high school. He was beginning to ask more in-depth questions about his adoption and communicated an interest in possibly locating his birth mother when he turned eighteen. Conflicted over their son's new interest in his birth family, they sought a consultation. In the parent interview, Amanda sheepishly expressed conflict with her husband. She revealed that they have known since they adopted Patrick that he has two older siblings who live with his birth mom. John firmly believes they should not tell their son until he asks them. John says firmly, "What good will it do? I am not sure we could find them and, anyway, Patrick never has asked if he has siblings."

Amanda feels she should not keep this from her son regardless of her husband's opinion. "I am ambivalent now because he may be angry with us that we waited so long to tell him. Also I worry about the fact that he may want to find them," says Amanda.

It became clear to the interviewer that both Amanda and John were afraid that Patrick might want to search for his birth siblings once he knew of their existence. They worried about what effect his efforts would have on their relationship with their son. John and Amanda acknowledged that they were also having a great deal of anxiety about Patrick leaving home. They feared, on some level, that their son would never come home once he left. The concept of their son even thinking about his birth family proved to be emotionally challenging for them. John and Amanda needed help to see how important the information they were holding was to Patrick. They were stuck in only seeing the issues as they related to them, not their son. The therapist worked with the parents to help them to feel safe enough to share the information with Patrick and provide support to help in the process of Patrick's transition to college and independence.

● ●

Attitude toward Birth Parents

During the assessment process it is also critical to explore the parental beliefs and attitudes toward the birth parents. The degree of openness in adoptions has greatly increased over the past two decades. Before that, a wall of secrecy existed between the new adoptive family and the child's biological parents. The birth mother was expected to forget the child she gave up for adoption. It was believed that the adoptive family provided a new start and the child should not be encumbered with past connections. This approach completely ignored children's developmental need to explore and incorporate their roots, a need that becomes intense in adolescence. Present practices vary widely between localities and even agencies in the same area. State laws also differ.

For these reasons, the diagnostician needs to explore a number of questions: What were the legal and agency expectations and rules regarding this adoption? Have the adoptive parents met the birth parents? What, if any, ongoing relationships do they have? What degree of openness was formally established in the adoption? Has the adopted teen grown up with regular contact with the birth family? Are there visits with the birth parents and/or siblings? Do they share letters and pictures? Even if there has been no active interaction, do they at least know how to contact the birth family if they wish to? If there was prior contact, what did they learn about the birth parents and extended birth family? Do they have pictures of the birth parents? How do they feel about the birth parents? If there was contact, how did the birth parents and the adoptee react to the reunion? All of these questions are of potential importance in any adoptive family, but particularly important in the family with youngsters who were adopted at later ages and who have had long and significant relationships with others prior to adoption.

● ●

CASE EXAMPLE

During the initial assessment Jocelyn mentioned that her son Raual was asking a lot more questions about his birth mother. He wanted to know what she was like, whether she finished school, and what she liked to do. Jocelyn told the therapist that she became extremely angry when her son began talking about his birth mom. She stated angrily, "I can't think of anything nice to say about her! She hurt my son. All the drugs she took almost killed him." Jocelyn explained that Raual's significant developmental and physical handicapping conditions were the result of his birth mother's drug use during her pregnancy.

The therapist acknowledged her conflicted feelings and explained to Jocelyn that no matter what happened in the past she must look deep into her heart to find some features of the birth mother that would be neutral or positive. The therapist explained that if drug use were her only defining

Beneath the Mask

trait, it would be the only part of his birth origin with which Raual could identify. Jocelyn shed tears and feared that she could not do what the therapist was suggesting. She was flooded with emotions of disgust and hate.

Raual's afflictions were a daily reminder of the choices his birth mother made — choices that had grave consequences. With several months of therapy and her son's expanding search for his legacy, Jocelyn was able to move beyond her own feelings and recognize the needs of her son. Jocelyn contacted the local child placement agency that placed Raual to seek any additional information that she could share with her son. Several weeks following the initial contact, the agency called and provided more information. Jocelyn learned that in high school Raual's birth mother was an accomplished artist and had won several awards. What proved to be quite powerful to Jocelyn was that Raual was also a fabulous artist. Stepping beyond her own convictions, Jocelyn was able to help her son see beyond his birth mother's addiction and the pain it caused him. She afforded her son the experience to weave a few positive threads from his birth mother within the fabric of his identity.

● ● ● ● ● ● ● ● ● ● ● ● ● ● ● ● ● ● ● ●

If the adoptive parents depict birth parents in a positive manner, it ultimately fosters more openness and paves the way for teens to share their thoughts and feelings about birth parents. Also, positive presentation of birth parents will promote a healthy integration of self as teens solidify their identity. This does not mean that birth parent problems cannot or should not be addressed. However, if issues of this nature are shared with the teen, the adoptive parents need to be sensitive to the impact on the adopted child. Severe problems can be presented with sympathy and understanding, especially if they are described in conjunction with some positive traits or accomplishments.

Whether the birth family is involved in the teen's life or not, the therapist should acquire as much information about the birth family as is feasible. This includes asking adoptive parents what knowledge they have about the birth parents, from a preadoptive perspective to exploring the relationship between the birth parents and individual birth parent history. It is useful to obtain any available data regarding the family of origin. The reasons surrounding the placement are critically important. For example, the question of whether relinquishment was voluntary or involuntary may play an important role in the process of adjustment to adoption. Naturally, any information about the pregnancy and other medical facts are valuable to the process of understanding the adopted child and his or her development. Finally, the details of the placement process, the actual physical transfer of the child, touch on powerful emotional issues of all parties and may open important areas for exploration.

The Dynamics of the Adoptive Family

As the therapist collects this variety of somewhat objective information, there is also an opportunity to reach some tentative conclusions about more subtle emotional currents in the adoptive family. For example, the therapist may begin to sense the strength or weakness of the adoptive family's sense of entitlement to parent this child. Do they have a deep-seated conviction of their right to parent this child? Many factors, including guilt about taking the child from the birth parent, personal shame and guilt over infertility, and possible ambivalence toward the commitment to adopt, can interfere with effective parenting. Too often, a compromised sense of entitlement fosters ineffectual parenting, which can be seen in lack of discipline, role confusion, and a family system without clear boundaries and expectations.

The therapist will also gain a sense of the extent to which the adoptive parents have claimed the child as truly a part of the family.

Parents and children need to express their feelings about being part of an adoptive family. This assessment includes extended family members who may support the creation of the adoptive family or who may criticize and question the decision to adopt.

Assessments with adoptees and their families must take into consideration the developmental stage of understanding and emotional processing of adoption in all members of the adoption circle: adoptees, birth parents, and adoptive parents. The therapist will want to assess how the family has approached the differences adoption has made to them (Nickman, 2004; Reitz and Watson, 1992).Adoption is a powerful emotional event producing inevitable changes in all family members. However, families vary widely in their emphasis on these changes. To briefly examine these differences, we offer the shorthand notion of the three B's.

1. Blind

   The adoptive parents communicate that adoption has been a wonderful experience for their family. "I can't imagine that any of the problems she is having are related in any way to adoption." "There are no differences," the parents declare. "We are so much alike that most people have no idea Sam is adopted. In fact his aunts and uncles often comment how much Sam looks like his dad." In these families, the adolescent's effort to talk about adoption or birth parents are brushed aside or may even be met with anger (Salomone, 2000).

2. Balanced

   The adoptive parents acknowledge the differences adoption brings and can discuss openly and honestly the compatibility issues inherent in adoption. "'We know that Samantha struggles with her racial identity. We try so very hard to support her and strive to be a multiracial family. We know there are times that she just cannot talk about this with us." In these families, open discussion of fantasies about birth parents, wishes to search for these parents, and even the limitations of the perceived compatibility between child and parents can be openly explored without any sense of danger to the basic bond between family members.

3. Blaming

These adoptive parents have a narrow range of perceived compatibility. They often exaggerate the importance of the adoptive status of their child, especially when problems arise or the teen does not live up to their wishes and expectations. Any shortcomings are explained on the basis of the adoption — rarely their own mistakes or flaws as parents. If the teen makes them feel good by doing something that is in sync with their expectations, they are more apt to claim their teen. Then they say, "He is my husband's son, made the honor roll again this semester." In contrast, when they are not pleased, the mother may be heard to say, "Your father was an incredible athlete. I don't understand why you are not interested in playing sports. Instead you keep signing up for all those ridiculous tryouts in the drama department." Parents may complain profusely to their therapist like this parent did: "Carlos is so very different from us that it's hard for us to connect with him. Our family has always excelled in sports. Why can't he see the importance in playing a team sport? If you ask me, I think he inherited laziness from his birth father."

ASSESSMENT OF THE ADOLESCENT

Once the clinician has interviewed the adoptive parents in detail and used their input to form tentative opinions about the particulars of this adoptive situation, it is time to talk with the adolescent. It will require empathy, tact, and perseverance for the therapist to obtain useful and accurate information about the direct experience of this central figure in the adoption drama. The very act of approaching the topic of adoption with adolescents is a delicate process.

Even if adolescents are from a "balanced" family — one in which open discussion of adoptive issues has been encouraged — they have often encountered uncomfortable responses from people outside the family, ranging from embarrassment and avoidance to outright insults. By adolescence, the adopted person has learned to be wary. In addition, of course, the adolescent may have personal reasons to be uncomfortable with the subject. If the youngster's family is either "blind" or "blaming," there are even more powerful reasons not to express one's feelings.

The ability to discuss the pertinent issues is also influenced by the adolescent's developmental maturity. Adoption is a profound experience affecting the adoptee at various developmental stages in his or her life. Age alone cannot guarantee the level of psychological maturation. The meaning of the adoptive experience is greatly influenced by the adolescent's evolving cognitive capacity. Most youngsters in the adolescent age range are capable of thinking and processing information in an abstract way. Adolescence, especially in its middle and late phases, is usually a time that emphasizes abstraction, imagination, and a battling of symbolic dragons. Because of this, earlier thoughts and questions about the adoption experience resurface in a more complex, sophisticated way.

In order to facilitate open discussion of the topic, it is important that the clinician is completely comfortable with the topic. (The process of assessing one's own biases regarding adoption and mastering them is discussed at length in chapter 2.) When this comfort is genuine, it is possible to communicate to the adolescent a readiness to explore the topic. Therapists can confidently state their knowledge and experience, which qualifies them to understand and help the adopted adolescent successfully travel his or her particular path.

It should not come as a surprise if the therapist senses defensiveness and even hostility in the interview with the adopted adolescent. The literature reports a common tendency for adoptees to believe that they were given away by the birth parent because there was something wrong with them. Often they feel that they are damaged goods. As Zuckerman and Buschbaum (2000) note in their excellent article "Strangers in a Strange Room," the adolescent's negative self-worth may result in the projection of disapproving and rejecting attitudes on the therapist. Needless to say, this expectation of a critical attitude does not improve the adolescent's cooperative attitude. Most adolescents are quick to dismiss therapists they feel are not forthright with them or lack the ability to approach them in a respectful and collaborative manner. They have well-tuned radar to detect therapists who can't walk the talk. The adopted adolescent often has overactive radar that detects attacks that have never been launched. The friendly approach of the examiner may lead to tossing depth charges, which must be survived if the therapist is to prove their status as an ally.

● ● ● ● ● ● ● ● ● ● ● ● ● ● ● ● ● ● ● ●

CASE EXAMPLE

Katia, a beautiful, engaging seventeen year old from eastern Europe, was accompanied by her mother and father following a drug overdose at school. Katia quickly informed the group of adults that she was not talking and that this was going to be waste of time for everyone, including herself. Katia's parents communicated that her increasingly hostile interactions with others was affecting her private school community and that her placement was tenuous. Katia had already been expelled from the local public school system for drug use. Katia was unconcerned. "Screw school! I didn't want to go there anyway," she said. Recognizing Katia's resistance, her parents were asked to describe briefly the reasons why Katia was being referred for therapy and then told to wait in the waiting area.

Now the therapist was alone with the furor of an unhappy teen. Katia abruptly stated, "I'm sick of coming to places like this — this is B.S. and you're just like the rest of them."

The therapist acknowledged Katia's rage and reflected on her need to self-medicate her pain. Katia seemed even angrier. "Why do you give a shit what I do with my anger? It's not your problem," she snapped.

"You're right," the therapist stated, "But it certainly seems to be a problem for you, as we would not be sitting here face to face if it wasn't. You know, Katia, I see lots of teenagers who are adopted and have very strong feelings about their adoption experience, and sometimes some difficult, painful things have happened to them."

Silence prevailed. Katia glared at the therapist for a while and then blurted out, "You would be pissed too if you had to leave your little sister and never said good-bye."

Katia was placed at age six from an orphanage. Her sister had been separated from her and sent to another orphanage. No adults shared that Katia had a younger sister, nor had Katia. She was living with this tremendous unresolved loss. For several years Katia had been living in a state of denial, protecting herself from the painful truth of her losses — the loss of her birth parents and her sister.

● ● ● ● ● ● ● ● ● ● ● ● ● ● ● ● ● ● ● ●

The Adoption Story

One straightforward and reasonable question that can be asked early in the interview relates to the simple facts of the adoption process. This question can help the adolescent delve into the issues. Many adoptive professionals and families refer to this information as one's adoption story. This query can be aired with or without parents present. In a family session, it is a good diagnostic tool for assessing the family's comfort level in speaking about the adoption, revealing valuable clues about how family members have communicated about the adoption over the years.

The telling of the adoption story sometimes shows that there have been important gaps in reporting or understanding. In some cases, it becomes evident that the parents have not adequately answered questions that have surfaced as the adoptee develops. Too often, information may have been shared, but due to the emotional charge of the information and/or the temperament or developmental age of the child, it was not processed and absorbed by the youngster. In fact, more often than not, the adolescent presents a story riddled with gaping holes. The parent may say, "Cassie, I told you that I did meet your birth mom when you were born and her name is Helen." The child may reply indignantly, "No, you didn't! You never told me you knew her name."

In the individual assessment interview with the adolescent, asking teens to describe their adoption story will often afford the therapist a very clear understanding of the comfort level of the family in relation to adoption as well as the teen's self understanding

● ●

CASE EXAMPLE

Nathan, fifteen years old, was referred after stealing his parents' car and getting arrested. In the family interview, he was asked about his adoption story. Nathan angrily said, "My best friend Luke told me in the woods behind my house when I was seven that I was adopted. I was blown away and really mad."

His mother asked him why he never discussed these feelings with her before and he turned to her and said, "Mom, how can I talk to you about my adoption? You wring your hands like you're doing now, your neck gets all red, and you start crying. There is no way I could talk to you about adoption." Then he added bitterly, "Worst of all, you lied to me! I hate you!"

Nathan's mom and dad wanted to protect their son from hurt and thought it would be better if he never knew he was abandoned by his birth father at a local grocery store. So much for the old notion that talking about adoption within the family might stir up trouble! That is true only if the trouble is already there. It is better not to ignore the fire burning in the basement. It will surely spread!

Once the story is shared, it becomes a road map that the therapist and the adolescent may now travel together in pursuit of understanding and acceptance.

● ●

Universalization and Education

Drawing from common adoption issues that other adopted adolescents have shared in therapy is another very effective approach in drawing out the adoption conflicts held by so many teens. Normalizing what the teen may be feeling, but is reluctant to share, paves the way for a more honest self-disclosure and safe discussion with the teen.

● ●

CASE EXAMPLE

Brent, age thirteen, came with his parents to the initial assessment after being referred by his guidance counselor concerned by his declining school performance and increasing social isolation. During the assessment the therapist asked, "Brent, what can you tell me about your adoption story, how you joined your family?"

Guarded and aloof, Brent turned to the therapist and said, "I never think about my adoption. I don't know why we are here and talking about this." Brent's mother spoke up and commented that lately he had made comments about wanting to know more about his birth parents, in particular his birth father. Brent looked angrily toward his mom and said, "So what is the big deal?"

The therapist commented that in some ways Brent is right. What is the big deal? The therapist explained that, in fact, most adopted teens his age have increasing thoughts and questions about their birth parents. The therapist added that most adopted kids have very deep feelings and questions about their birth parents.

Brent looked surprised and revealed that he sometimes feels guilty thinking about birth parents since he has two parents who he knows love him. To think of his other family caused Brent to feel disloyal to his adoptive family.

● ●

These guilt feelings, which are common, can make adoption conversations with parents extremely uncomfortable and create barriers within the therapeutic process if not addressed. Another effective strategy to open the interchange is educating the adoptee as to the normal developmental issues inherent in adoption during adolescence. Often it is wise to do this *before* asking about the youngster's personal experience. Using an educational approach can be a powerful tool because it can bolster the adolescent's sense of empowerment through the acquisition of knowledge. Adolescence as a developmental period brings with it a desire for information. Knowledge promotes the feeling of being in control of self and the world, an experience that reduces anxiety and breeds confidence. (In chapter 4 we explore more about control as an important clinical issue in adoption.)

ʙeneath the мask

A reasonable approach is to state, "Our experience here has taught me that there is a whole range of feelings in young people about their adoption." The therapist then describes typical feelings and thoughts that teens do have about their adoption experience. This shows the adolescent that feelings are predictable and related to the experience of adoption, and not due to some peculiarity in them. The experience of adoption leads naturally to some human reactions, which, though sometimes extreme, are quite normal.

Remember Matthew from a previous case example? Let's see how educating Matthew helped him to move beyond his shame and guilt as he pondered the reasons for his relinquishment. Matthew truly believed that he *must* have done something to cause his mother not to keep him. He is not unlike many adoptees we have treated at C.A.S.E who feel solely responsible for their relinquishment. Their reasoning goes like this: Look at me, I'm the exception, not the rule. All parents keep their children. There must be a reason why my parent did not want to keep me. Matthew needed to be educated that feeling responsible is a common phenomenon among adoptees, particular among adopted teens. We know that the abandonment felt by the adoptee can lead to shame-based identity (Gulden and Bartels-Rabb, 1993).

The teen's sense of personal inadequacy must be challenged by our information. Every day our clinicians encounter shame-based adolescents who have carried the burden for relinquishment on their shoulders for some time. The weight of this responsibility is overwhelming and unnecessary. The task during the assessment process with Matthew was to reeducate him in order to begin to help him be relieved of his sense of guilt and shame. He was flatly told there is no way that any adoptee that we ever have met did anything to cause a relinquishment. Relinquishment is purely about adult situations and choices.

Another useful educational technique is to draw from common adoption issues that other adopted adolescents have shared in therapy. If that previous patient, "Johnny" or "Tamara," had serious adoption conflicts, it may help the current teen to hear their stories. Using books that depict adoptees' feelings is another valuable tool.

With the information obtained from a careful assessment, the clinician is ready to begin the process of trying to understand the complexities of adoption within a therapeutic framework. The developmental history underlines the tasks that face the adopted adolescent. As the therapeutic journey proceeds, there are key developmental adoption tasks to complete:

1. Understanding the reasons underlying the relinquishment.

2. Supporting teens as they come to grips with these reasons. Even if the adopted child cannot completely forgive the birth parents, this effort, including expressions of anger and sadness, may help to resolve loss issues.

3. Acknowledging that there are two sets of parents and integrating adoption into the teen's identity.

The journey is not traveled in isolation. Adoptive parents must follow the journey with their adolescents by helping them to gain a deeper understanding of why they were adopted. It is the parents' responsibility to impart as much information as is available to assist young people in the integration of self. The adoptive parent must also give permission to grieve the losses and be there to support the mourning process. Often it is necessary to give permission for their adoptive teens to be openly curious about the birth parents. This will include accepting that adolescents need to think about, talk about, and possibly search for their birth family (Kirk, 1964). The work ahead is challenging; it presents many hurdles to overcome.

*It's not fair that I cannot know where I came from, where
certain traits are from, or who I look like.*
Becca

CHAPTER 4

Adolescent stuck spots

six major Hurdles for the Adopted Adolescent

To assist clinicians who provide therapy to adopted adolescents, C.A.S.E. has identified the six most common adoption related issues where children and adolescents may get stuck. Although not all teens may be affected by each "stuck spot," our experience has shown us that it is very common for them to move in and out of each area as they try to gain deeper understanding of their personal adoption experience. Remember, early in the assessment process it is often difficult to ascertain the extent to which adoption is a variable in the presenting symptomatology. Using these issues as a road map may help therapists to develop a responsive treatment plan that will embrace the key issues inherent in adoption.

REASON FOR ADOPTION
Therapy with children involves helping them to have greater understanding as to why they were placed for adoption and to clarify information about their adoption story. Children need to know that they

are not responsible for the decisions surrounding their relinquishment — that adoption occurs because of adult decisions. Children may need assistance in both identifying and coming to terms with their feelings related to their adoption experience.

The minds of adopted teens are filled with questions like these: Why was I given away? Was there something wrong with me? Did they give me away because they did drugs or abused me? What does this mean about me? Why couldn't they have worked things out and taken care of me?

Nothing highlights these questions better than some of the artwork our clients do as part of their therapy. As you walk into one of the counseling rooms at C.A.S.E., there is a large drawing hung on the wall that quickly catches your eye. The picture is filled with colorful question marks, some small, some very large. At the bottom, scripted in youthful writing are the words, "Why was I adopted?" In another room a similar message: a picture of a young girl sitting alone on her bed holding a piece of paper with a bright pink question mark. The caption on the bottom of this drawing says, "Why didn't they want me?" In another room taped to the wall is a poster with the words, "Why Was I Adopted?" in blue and green. Beside it the same question is written by a different hand in different colors. The prevalence of this overwhelming theme reflects the depth of the children's bewilderment regarding their abandonment. (See figure 4.1 and 4.2 in appendix A.)

Prior to adolescence, adopted children are extremely curious about their adoption story. Although they question the circumstances that led to their adoption, most of them seem to accept the answers calmly, if somewhat sadly. Sometimes they lack the cognitive development to truly understand all the ramifications of what they are told. Sometimes adoptive parents sweeten the story or omit painful details.

In adolescence, the tone of the questioning changes and assumes a new dimension for the adoptee. Adolescents often demand fuller

Beneath the Mask

and more factual answers, and they often respond with anger as they reflect on their abandonment. The older youngster now understands that most mothers love, nurture, and protect their babies. Why not in their case? Was there something wrong with her? Was there something terribly wrong with him? They are quietly or openly preoccupied with these questions.

As more sophisticated critical thinkers, adolescents refine their earlier vague questions into the very personal and painful exploration of the question "Why did my birth mother and birth father leave *me*?" The phrases "leave me," "reject me," "abandon me," "give me away," and the like echo in the minds of many adopted teens. As Nydam says in his powerful book *Adoptees Come of Age* (1999), "Nothing hurts like relinquishment hurts." Since adolescents rarely suffer in silence but often do not disclose the true source of their suffering, the result is often a furious, irritable, and very difficult young person.

To make things more difficult, this begins very early in adolescence, a period of heightened upheaval and confusion for most youngsters. The already stressed adopted adolescent reconnects with the powerful awareness that to have been adopted, someone had to give them away. They wonder if they ever were loved in the first place. They also realize that the people who hurt them so badly are out there someplace. That is a strange thought. Their speculations about these "other parents" are endless. Do they regret losing me? Do they miss me? Are they glad they don't have to bother with me?

Sometimes the adolescent is just blindly enraged about what was done to them. Cournos (2004) has written about the experience both from her thirteen-year-old perspective and her view as a professional adult. Her observations provide a useful guide to those of us who are trying to help. Elyse provides a more raw and immediate view in her poem "Your Fault."

YOUR FAULT

It's your entire fault
For causing this pain
You destroyed my life
It's not a game
It's all your fault
I turned out this way
Now I am stuck with this feeling day to day
It's all your fault
It's your entire fault for making me feel so sad.

During the initial phases of writing this book, we carefully reviewed hundreds of cases, trying to extrapolate common themes that were represented in the treatment profiles of our adolescent population. We became acutely aware of the high percentage of teens who were struggling to find ways to heal from the powerful injury caused by their relinquishment. In her book *The Primal Wound* (1993) adoptive parent and social worker Nancy Verrier describes the narcissistic injury that occurs at the time of relinquishment. She reflects on the imprinting of this injury upon the unconscious mind of children. Verrier asserts that this injury "affects the adoptee's sense of self and often manifests in a sense of loss, basic trust, anxiety and depression, emotional and or behavioral problems, and difficulties in relationships with significant others" (21). The mental health literature has repeatedly reported research that clearly shows that the loss of a loved one, particularly a parent, is one of the most painful and damaging experiences a person can experience. It is even more disruptive if the loss occurs during childhood. It is interesting that the death of a parent is less harmful to future development than voluntary separation such as divorce or abandonment (Kendler et al., 1992). We must never forget that adoption begins with and is built upon just such a loss.

Kirk (1964) has referred to the "involuntary migration" that is forced on the adopted child.

No matter how we wish to dismiss this predication, the truth is that adoption is not possible without loss. The adoptee has lost the opportunity to grow up with their biological family; the infertile adoptive parents have lost the possibility of a biological child and their genetic continuity; the birth parents have lost the child born to them. Because the issues of grief and loss are such a prominent factor in the treatment issues of the children and adolescents that we see, we began to review adoption literature in search of therapeutic frameworks to help adoptees resolve grief and loss issues.

Grief work has been conceptualized in many ways, beginning with the pioneering work of Dr. Kubler-Ross. Understanding the different stages of grief one may pass through as proposed by Kubler-Ross (1969), Bourguignon, and Watson (1987) does provide a framework for understanding how an individual reacts to loss, but it falls short of embracing the loss in adoption. For the loss in adoption *is* unique from all other losses. Loss in adoption does not have closure as in death; in adoption the loss is potentially reversible and flooded with ambiguity. The birth family is out there somewhere — in Romania, Siberia, Guatemala, Texas, Maryland, somewhere. Things are not final.

Another characteristic of loss in adoption is it is less socially recognized. As a society, we embrace adoption in a celebratory way because we believe that all children have the right to be in a permanent loving family. Adoption is embraced as a happy event that should be celebrated, not mourned. Looking clear-eyed at the many losses behind this happy scene might spoil the warm and fuzzy glow. However, not looking will lead to later and greater pain.

If we, as professionals, acknowledge that adoption is built upon a foundation of loss, it becomes our responsibility to help families resolve their grief. We will receive little help from general society. There are virtually no codified rituals to help adopted youngsters to express and resolve their pain. This deficiency is unfortunate since the loss in adoption is pervasive and lifelong. The individual does not suffer each day of his life, but our clinical experience has shown us that loss issues in adoption will resurface at key developmental and prominent life transitional periods. These include entering adolescence, leaving home, marriage, pregnancy, and childbirth, as well as traumatic events such as loss of a current loved one or major life disappointments.

● ●

CASE EXAMPLE

Lily, age seventeen, was referred for therapy following a theft of a student's wallet at school. Lily had also been suspended numerous times for behavioral issues. She was separated from her biological family at age five and placed in an orphanage due to abuse and neglect as a result of alcoholism in the birth family. Lily was adopted from Latvia at the age of eight. Entering therapy, Lily presented herself as very guarded, noncommunicative, and hostile. It was clear that she had no intention of speaking to anyone about herself and that her business was her business.

Week after week Lily came into the therapist's office, stared out the window, and responded minimally to questions posed to her. Finally, tired of "wasting" her time, Lily responded to one of many explorative questions. This one happened to be about friends. Lily revealed that a very close friend died two years ago from leukemia and that people wanted her to talk about it, but she was not going to.

She said, "It's history; I don't know why everyone is making such a big deal about it." Lily quickly closed up tight as a clam and pronounced the session over. The following week Lily came in fit for a fight and stated that she did not know why she told the therapist about her friend. She ordered the therapist not to ask anymore about her. The therapist empathetically responded to Lily and told her that she felt sad that Lily had lost so many people in her life. Lily remained aloof.

In the next session the therapist delicately broached the friend subject again. With tears in her eyes Lily said that her friend was her soul mate. She was just like her in many ways, and she was the only person to whom Lily had told everything. Lily began to talk about the fact that she had very few close relationships and kept most very superficial. The therapist asked why she thought it was scary to let others close, and Lily said, "No one wants me. My real mother didn't want me either! There were only two people who I cared about and they both left me!"

This time Lily did not retreat. She slowly allowed herself to reach into a place within which had been darkened by fear. Fear of the unknown, fear of the known. Lily had some early memories of her birth parents. These memories were mostly wrought with pain and a few lit by happiness. Lily struggled with depending on someone to guide her through the darkness. She did not trust that anyone would stick with her. Gradually and cautiously she deepened her trust in the therapist and accepted support to grieve her losses.

● ●

Unfortunately, while we take justifiable pride in celebrating adoption, we must also afford children an opportunity to express their grief and mourn such powerful losses. There are few suggestions in the adoption literature for how therapists can help children through their bereavement. There are also few materials to help adoptive parents to recognize the signs of unresolved loss and hidden grief in their angry and belligerent adopted adolescent. There is also little available to help them understand the grief connected to adoption and the ways that they can assist their child in the process of facing and resolving loss issues. This is a tragic deficiency since we know with great certainty that losses that are not mourned are debilitating, freezing the individual in a state of uncertainty and angry ambiguity.

As a result, the adolescent enters therapy with a myriad of behavioral symptoms and feelings associated with unresolved grief. Unresolved grief and loss can and will manifest into maladaptive symptomatology if not addressed. Grief that is not grieved will root itself and surface at some point in the adoptee's life. We must afford the adolescent the opportunity to affirm, mourn, and manage these profound losses. We must remember that one's reaction to relinquishment is not static but rather flows through the life journey of the adoptee.

Unfortunately, the majority of the teens who present therapeutically are disconnected from the source of their pain. They need support and a well-planned treatment approach if they are to identify and manage the grief embedded in their relinquishment. It is critical that the treating clinician explore with teens how they "experience" the relinquishment, remembering that the loss of the parent is the most devastating of all losses. We also need to remember that of all losses experienced in relationships, ambiguous loss is the most devastating. Due to the ambiguity of the situation, the individual often feels confused and distressed. The longer the ambiguity persists, the greater the impact upon the child's sense of personal mastery and competency. It is impossible for them to resolve the issues of loss, as there is no finality to the situation. Adopted adolescents can become immobilized. They cannot begin to grieve when the loss is indeterminate and only partly recognized.

CASE EXAMPLE

Lynn, age nineteen, was adopted at age three from the Philippines and knew very little about her birth family other than that her birth mother died after childbirth and her birth father was extremely poor. Reportedly, Lynn had become very ill. Recognizing he could not care for his daughter, her father took her to a missionary, who provided proper care and saved her life.

Lynn entered therapy at the age of eleven with symptoms of depression and increasing levels of anxiety. She was struggling in school, becoming agitated with peers, and having difficulty maintaining relationships. During the initial stages of therapy Lynn revealed that she thought a lot about her birth father and brother and wondered how they were. Lynn remembers having an older brother; however, there was never any confirmation of this during the placement. Lynn confided that while these thoughts have persisted, she is afraid to talk about them with her parents as she worries about hurting their feelings. Lynn believed that her parents would feel she did not love them if they knew she was still thinking about her birth family.

Week after week Lynn would come to therapy describing distressing dreams about the day her father and brother took her to the airport and said goodbye to her as she left for America to be adopted. Lynn recalled memories of her brother holding her hand not wanting to let her go. She also recalls not wanting to let go of him. It is important to note that there is no confirmation that they were actually present.

Her losses were profound and overwhelmingly hard for her to manage. She began to get in touch with her grief surrounding the loss of her birth family. It became evident that her depression and anxiety were driven by insurmountable unresolved grief as well as the fear that abandonment could happen again. Lynn had worked hard to suppress her feelings, but they captured her unconscious mind, flooding her dreams and turning them into nightmares. As the grief remained unresolved, Lynn began engaging in self-mutilating behaviors, cutting her arms, face, and legs. This was just one of the symptoms that brought her to treatment. The pain of her losses became too much to bear.

Lynn described her grief as a tidal wave that swept her away to a place she could not swim back from. Her feelings of sadness prevailed, destroying any chance she could reap joy from her surroundings. Lynn remained isolated at home and at school with ambivalent attachment to her parents. Her early memories of her relinquishment continued to invade her consciousness. In therapy she wept because she would never know her birth mother, who was now dead. She was preoccupied with her desire to one day find her birth father and brother.

Therapy has been a key support system for Lynn and her parents, and together they have made considerable progress. Lynn has remained in therapy through all these years, sometimes taking breaks when she feels stable. However, the loss issues tend to resurface during periods of high stress in her life. These include the beginning of the school year, midsemester grading periods, holidays, changes in the student community in her school, and conflicts with the friends she is beginning to connect with. Whenever Lynn begins to feel uncertain about herself and her surroundings, she starts to fear abandonment by others close to her, including her parents. She continues periodically to question her life's purpose, her sense of competency, and her self-worth. She fears that bad things will continue to happen in her life and that in some way she deserves this. She sometimes expresses the belief that she should have never been rescued by the missionaries. It has been very difficult for her to heal from her traumatic beginnings and her profound losses.

● ●

As C.S. Lewis (1976) said, "I never knew grief would feel so much like fear!" Indeed, all too often, Lynn is engulfed by fear. Having a safe, consistent therapeutic setting with a therapist who is familiar with the pain of adoptive loss for the past eight years of her life has afforded her the support and understanding that allows her to bear her pain and continue to grow. Total resolution may or may not be possible in time. Lynn, now age nineteen, wrote this poem to reflect her growth and healing.

I AM LUCKy

I am Lucky
The Lucky Girl
Is Me
Someone who has two families
In the past and the Future
One family is Gone
And the other family is alive
I am lucky
The Lucky girl is me
Someone who has love in my heart and mind
How kind...How kind
I have Cousins
I have uncles

I have aunts
I have mom and Dad
And also Grandma and Grandpa
This family is still living with me
But the other family
Who is in the past
Will always be in my heart
And that memory will never fall apart
I am lucky
The lucky Girl
Is me
I have people who love me.

This case demonstrates that sometimes the most important message in the therapy of teen adoptees who are so flooded by uncertainty and rejection is helping them to see that not everyone will leave them. Plain old stubborn persistence is often what is prescribed. Adolescents need ongoing proof that the therapist will not guide them to a place of pain and then desert them. Therapists must prove that they can and will walk along this journey with them and can hold their fear and profound grief. They must feel safe in order to express their confusion as to how their birth mother and birth father could walk away from their parental responsibilities. As one twelve-year-old said to me, "Mothers keep their babies. Why didn't she keep me?"

In addition to refusing to be pushed away, it is also important to normalize their feelings. Let them know that other teens who are adopted also feel ambivalent about securing attachments, fear that people will leave them, and that it is unsafe to get close. At C.A.S.E. we spend a great deal of time affirming and legitimizing the prevalence of these feelings. Because adolescents can think in a more sophisticated manner, you can dialogue with them in an educative style, helping them to understand the origins of these feelings. This information will assist them in acquiring some understanding as to

Beneath the Mask

why they hold such conflicted feelings and thoughts about getting close to others. Once they grasp this insight, then they are more willing to be guided to recognize and explore the strategies they have employed to keep others at bay. The goal, of course, is to avoid a repeated separation and rejection, an all too familiar pattern frequently triggered by the youngster's attachment problems. Adoptees live with what Nydam (1999) calls "relinquishment sensitivity." According to Nydam (1999, 17), "relinquishment sensitivity has to do with a special sense of hurt that accompanies rejection in its many forms. This sensitivity may be disguised by anger or depression, but the underlying hurt, reminiscent of the primal wound of relinquishment, is the most basic factor."

Though adoptees are often totally unaware of their unconscious fear of abandonment and the accompanying sensitivity to relinquishment, this basic vulnerability still causes anxiety, depression, and hypervigilance. These adopted youngsters will go to the furthest extremes to ward off any possibility of being rejected.

MISSING OR DIFFICULT INFORMATION

As children make sense of their stories, they begin to confront the losses surrounding adoption experience. We must help children cope with difficult information, such as birth parent histories of abuse/neglect, substance abuse, mental illness, incarceration, or death. Adopted children often have to face the sad reality that there is information they would like to know, but it is unobtainable.

They may say, "I don't know what my birth parents looked like. I don't even have a picture of them." And they may ask questions like these: "Why was I abandoned?" "What's my real birthday?" "Do I have any brothers or sisters?" "Did my birth father care about my birth mother or was it a one-night stand?"

Younger adopted children are comfortable living with broad, generalized concepts of their birth parents. Adolescent adoptees seek the facts — the *detailed* facts. They want definite information about why and how they came to be relinquished. They want concrete and specific information about the appearance, personality, and lives of the people who conceived and brought them into this world.

Adoptive parents, in contrast, may be very hesitant to share information that they regard as potentially upsetting or damaging to the youngsters they love. It is important for therapists to understand and acknowledge this risk but to help parents to see that these risks are outweighed by the risks of not providing information. That void often gives rise to the fantasies regarding birth parents — fantasies that may be more damaging to identity formation than any facts could be. In addition, the adolescent's anger over being kept in the dark can poison the relationship with adoptive parents. In almost all cases, the truth — even if initially disturbing — frees youngsters and allows them to spend their energies in more productive ways.

Therapists are often asked for advice on the correct timing for sharing birth origin and relinquishment information with children. Experience has taught us that there are no cookbook answers to those questions. Each child's temperament and emotional and intellectual maturity will influence the readiness for processing this sometimes distressing information about the self. However, we are making decisions about the adolescent's personal possession — his or her life history. Certainly by adolescence, parents should reveal all details they know regarding the young person's adoption story. The risks of providing this information to the maturing adolescent are diminished by the adolescent's cognitive capacity to process information and newfound openness to considering facts and feelings through many different lenses.

● ●

CASE EXAMPLE
Adam was placed at birth. As he passed through childhood, his parents steadily provided him with pieces of his adop-

tion story. However, there was one fact they did not share. Adam's father was killed in a boating accident two months before Adam was born. Adam's parents had revealed basically everything about Adam's birth mother, but stayed clear of the birth father's death, fearing a possible negative impact. When Adam was fifteen, his parents asked for a consultation about the proper course to take regarding this gap in Adam's knowledge.

The parents were reassured that it was common for families to discuss birth mothers more than birth fathers. They were also told that the belief that birth fathers are not important to the adoption decision and have little interest in their children is widespread and has been perpetuated over time. However, the therapist pointed out that adopted teens are actually very interested in learning about their birth fathers. Normal adolescent concerns about dating, sexual identity, and moral standards in the sexual area are heavily influenced by paternal characteristics. The importance of this information to boys like Adam may be obvious, but adopted girls are equally curious about their birth fathers.

The therapist explained to Adam's parents that their son might have thoughts about his birth father but was keeping them to himself since his birth father had never been mentioned to him. They were strongly encouraged to share the information they had. The therapist also pointed out that the birth father's death might even have contributed to the decision to relinquish Adam. The parents were told that Adam's capacity for abstraction and his understanding of human behavior would help him to make constructive use of this crucial fact about his origins. Of course, the therapist also continued to recognize the parents' extreme anxiety about entering into this subject matter with their son. It was important to provide support and understanding but also encouragement to them to do what was best for Adam. The therapist agreed that this information would cause Adam anxiety and pain but that their willingness to tolerate his discomfort and to stay with him while he processed his reaction would help him to move forward stronger than ever. Parents do not need to take away pain. They need to acknowledge it and sit lovingly with the suffering child.

Adam's parents went home to contemplate their choices about if and when they were going to share this information with their son. Several weeks later they called and asked if they could come in again to discuss their decisions. The parents informed the therapist that they wished to bring their son in to talk about all of this and sought advice as to how to introduce the notion to Adam. The therapist had several individual sessions with Adam exploring what he knew about his story and the thoughts and questions he may have as a teenager about his adoption experience. Adam was curious about what extra information his parents had; he had suspected for a while they were holding something from him. Adam felt that it had something to do with his birth father since they never brought him up.

After some preparation work with the parents and Adam separately, a joint session was held in which Adam's parents acknowledged that they had some more information about his story. They said they hadn't known when to tell him but learned from the therapist that the information is his to know. The parents proceeded to tell Adam about his birth father. Adam tried to quietly process his parents' words and started to cry. He shared that he knew something was wrong because no one wanted to talk about his birth father. Adam understood why his parents hadn't shared this with him up until now, but he felt a little angry that they waited so long. "I have been thinking about him from time to time and thought I might want to find him one day. I guess that is never going to happen now."

Adam chose to continue therapy for a while to work on his feelings surrounding the death of his birth father and the questions it raised for him surrounding his relinquishment. Adam always wondered why his birth parents did not keep him and now suspects that due to his birth father's death, his birth mom could not parent alone. Though sad about his loss, Adam is relieved that he has been given the crucial part to his story that his parents carried. He realizes there are other pieces of missing information, which he may obtain later in his life. Adam's parents also feel relieved, as they had become uncomfortable holding on to this information but did not know how and when to share it. "It was extremely helpful to share our ambivalence and get advice from an adoption expert who knew how to help us. We were feeling so guilty yet wanted to protect our son. Our therapist helped us all along this journey," the parents wrote later in a thank-you note.

● ●

CASE EXAMPLE

Abby's parents came in for a consultation initiated by her mother. The mom was having increased anxiety about that fact that she and her husband knew that Abby's birthday was not her *real* birthday. Their daughter had been adopted from Russia, and the authorities there told them to just pick a birthday for her. They chose May 4. Several years later they gained additional information and learned that her actual birthday was December 14 of the previous year. This was fine when she was a young girl, but as she matured it became obvious that she appeared older and more developed than her presumed age.

Mom could no longer harbor the secret and wanted advice on how to best tell Abby the truth. There were problems in coming clean on the subject. The extended family always held a family reunion in May. Traditionally, Abby's birthday was celebrated at the gathering. The parents worried about the reaction of all Abby's relatives, who had been part of this joyful tradition for years.

Still, the parents strongly felt that Abby deserved the truth about her own life. After some therapeutic assistance they were able to let go of their guilt about keeping the secret and master their anxiety about everyone's reaction — especially Abby's. They agreed on a plan to reveal the facts to Abby, the family, and Abby's peers.

Abby's response to the news amazed and delighted them. She told them that she had been secretly worried that something was wrong with her. She wondered why her body was more mature than her friends. She was teased at times during sleepover parties because of her greater maturity. It was a great relief to learn that she was older than she had thought.

● ● ● ● ● ● ● ● ● ● ● ● ● ● ● ● ● ● ● ●

Abby's case illustrates again that no matter how difficult the parents may believe the facts to be, the adolescent may well have created even more disturbing fantasies about the missing information. Often adolescents embrace the new information and move it constructively into their sense of self.

Family therapy literature has often described the power of family secrets. In adopted families they can be even more destructive. The secrets withheld from the adopted youngster may be key building blocks for the young person's identity. As Betty Jean Lifton (1994, 23) so poignantly says, "The secret in the adoptive family is not that the child is adopted but who the child is."

DIFFERENCE

Feeling different from peers is the worst curse of adolescence. Nowhere along the developmental stages of life do people so desperately want to fit in, to be a part of the group, as they do in adolescence.

Being adopted creates a sense of being different in many ways. Adoptees may have a different appearance than their adoptive family, may have a different race or cultural background than their family, and may feel different from peers who are being raised in biologically related families. Feelings about these differences, if not addressed, can negatively affect a child's sense of self-worth and security with the adoptive family.

David Kirk, one of the pioneers in adoption studies, writes in *Shared Fate* (1954) about the importance of acknowledging the differences between adoptive parenting and biological parenting. These differences, if not acknowledged by the adoptive family, can lead to a rejection of the teen's differences. (Recall the "blind family" — the one who does not see how adoption does create differences — mentioned in chapter 2.

> *When I was younger I use to think everyone was adopted. My parents would take us to these gatherings where there were other adoptive families. My parents would say, 'See, all these kids are adopted just like you!' As I grew up it seemed that we saw less and less of these families who were supposedly just like us. It didn't take me long to figure out that not everyone was adopted like me. Now, I'm sixteen, and I am the only adopted person among my friends. I am different — being adopted means you are different.*

Adolescent stuck spots

These feelings were shared by Amy, who attended an adoption group for teens. Amy joined the group after telling her parents one night that she wished she never was adopted.

Differences in Appearance and Culture

In biological families, resemblances are taken for granted. In adoptive families, differences, particularly racial differences, are in the forefront. During adolescence, when self-identity is a major focus, many transracially adopted teens step toward the obscure culture of their birth parents, leaving behind the culture of their adoptive family.

●　●

CASE EXAMPLE

Pedro was referred for therapy by his parents when they became deeply concerned about their son's discomfort with being in a transracial family. "I feel I am one of those signs with flashing yellow lights — the fact that my skin color is different from my family's draws attention no matter where we are." Pedro was adopted at the age of eighteen months from Guatemala and grew up in a fairly diverse neighborhood.

During therapy Pedro shared that he hated living with a white family. "It used to be okay but now as I am older it seems more complicated." Pedro spoke of purposely walking way in front of his family when they were out in public because he felt embarrassed. "Sometimes to avoid questions from others I tell them that the woman who came to pick me up is our neighbor, not my white mother," he said.

Although Pedro's parents evaluated their ability to parent transracially and believed that they were doing all the right things, they may have minimized the power of the outside world's bias and racism. Furthermore, they did not grasp the power of the peer group in accepting their son.

What was missing for Pedro was a repertoire of survival skills necessary to combat the discrimination still evident in society and the misunderstandings about transracial adoption.

Therapy helped support Pedro to communicate his struggles as he himself tried to integrate his cultural, racial, and ethnic identity. Pedro's parents had no idea of the depth of racism he was experiencing. Therapy opened lines of communication around a topic that most of us still have difficulty speaking about. The family had to see themselves as a multiracial, multicultural, and multiethnic family. Pedro's parents were alarmed by the situations their son spoke of and the difficult questions he was often bombarded with. The therapist helped the entire family acquire skills to respond to these racial challenges and provide support and understanding to Pedro, who had been carrying his internal strife alone. It was now safe to speak about the unspeakable.

● ●

For many teens, challenges surface as they grow within a transracial family. Matthew, now twenty-four, entered therapy at age thirteen when challenged by a myriad of adoption issues. Matthew continues to seek the support of his therapist from time to time and agreed to share his thoughts now that he's a young man. In the following case example Matthew discusses his experiences as he looks back on his childhood and reflects on the differences he experienced in a multicultural, multiracial family.

CASE EXAMPLE

"Growing up as a kid my family seemed no different to me than any other. Mom was Mom, Dad was Dad, and my brother and sisters filled their respective roles as siblings. The fact that I was 'mixed,' as it was referred to then, or 'biracial,' as it is more commonly dubbed today, mattered little to me. The fact that my younger sister and both of my parents were white, and my younger brother was Korean mattered little to me. However, as I would soon come to realize, the fact that my older sister was biracial like myself, and could pass for a 'real' honest-to-goodness sibling upon first glance, mattered immensely.

"I was not aware of the apparent awkwardness my family's racial consistency thrust upon society at large until I reached my teenage years and was stripped of my naiveté. Up until that point, I knew my family *looked* different from my friends' families, but the feelings I witnessed in other family settings were identical to my own experiences. Internally, I always just assumed that there were other families out there that looked like mine — I just hadn't come across any yet.

Many of my friends knew that I was adopted and that I came from an adoptive family. It was never something that was hushed or swept under the rug. It was never a big deal to my friends, and in turn I never thought too much about it — as I thought it was quite normal. However, in efforts to make things even more comfortable, and perhaps lessen the perceived awkwardness that our family might put out, my older sister and I used our racial similarity to our advantage. We used to always tell people — even our closest friends — that we were 'real' brother and sister; that we were adopted together. At least that way we were able to pretend there was a biological link; that there was something there stronger than simply insisting against inquisitive minds that our family *was* a real family.

"To outsiders, however, outside my circle of friends and my family's, I soon came to realize the awkwardness that

BENEATH THE MASK

seemed to take people by surprise. When I began to flirt with the age of reason — somewhere around twelve or thirteen — I began to notice more things. It's said that when you're a kid, you notice everything. Though that may be true, when you're a kid, you are ill-equipped with the tools to decipher everything you notice. When you're a kid and you see someone you are unfamiliar with looking at you or your family, you don't think of them as *staring*, or staring in confusion, curiosity, or disgust. You just think that they are *looking*.

"As I got older, the looks became more noticeable and began to take on a different form. Soon, looks that I once classified as just that turned into scowls or disgust and visual admonishments. What we presented the world with when our family went out was this: two white adults old enough to be grandparents, a little white girl, an Asian baby, and two black children. This is my family as it looks to the world. I eventually became adept at reading the looks from strangers as we ventured out in public. Usually the looks we received went something like this: first, an initial glance, no different than I'd imagine you or I would receive if we walked into a room alone for the first time (but this is where the similarities end). Next would be the double take or the "what the hell?!" look. This was commonly followed by rapid eye movement on the part of the onlooker, from my parents, to my brother, to my sisters, to me in unlimited combinations, while they desperately tried to figure out the relationships between this strange group of people.

Finally, when onlookers finally did manage to figure out the relationships and identify us as a family, what followed were looks of shock, disgust, further curiosity, or a combination of this. This sequence of looks was something that I was soon able to feel without even visually observing. When all six of us walked into a restaurant, I could *feel* the stares of inquiring eyes. I no longer needed to witness our family being observed to know what was happening. After experiencing social acknowledgment that my family was "different" for the millionth time, I did not need to bear witness to it any longer. I was just resigned to deal with it since there was nothing I could do to change it.

"The fact that society holds my family as 'different' because we are an adoptive family — and different still because we are a biracial and multicultural family — is something that I have learned to live with. I've learned simply to ignore society's constant attempt to label our family as different. I *know* we are different than the typical family. I know we *look* different than the typical family. And after having society tell me so for so long, I've also learned that there's nothing I can do to make society stop staring. Ignoring the stares is how I've chosen to deal with it. Others, like my older sister, tend not to be patient and will voice their frustrations. However, I have chosen a less confrontational and perhaps less honorable means by which to deal with differentness. I acknowledge it, I accept it, and I deal with it. I don't ignore the fact that my family is different from the majority of families. What I ignore is the reminder that society gives me each and every day telling me so."

● ●

Peer Differences

We are all aware how vitally important peers are during the developmental stage of adolescence. Ask any adolescent — they would do anything for their friends and their friends would do anything for them. For transracially adopted teens, this sense of belonging and loyalty may be challenging to achieve.

CASE EXAMPLE

Katherine entered high school at age fourteen, and after the first few weeks of school her mother noticed that she seemed unhappy and withdrawn. Katherine's mom approached her but got the typical teen response: "Nothing is wrong!" Several weeks later, Katherine was caught drinking alcohol. Scared that her daughter was in trouble, mom brought her to therapy.

After getting past the typical adolescent attitude of "I don't know why my mom brought me here — nothing is wrong. So what if I got caught drinking? Everyone does it," Katherine was asked to speak about her friends. What were they like? Did she have a best friend? How has the transition from middle school to high school been? Katherine became teary eyed and said that she was really having a hard time. Katherine had made a personal decision to try to become more involved with the Korean peer group at her school. Unlike her brother, who was also adopted, she very much wanted to connect more with her cultural/ethnic origins.

Katherine said that, for the past month, she has been going to the cafeteria and sitting at the table where the Korean girls would congregate. Katherine described being flatly rejected as soon as they realized she really wasn't "Korean," meaning that she couldn't speak the language. "I knew very little about their culture — the only thing we had in common was *I looked like them.*"

Therapy afforded Katherine the opportunity to talk about her feelings of rejection and her strong need to learn more about her Korean identity and to be with peers who looked like her. We explored together ideas that might draw the teens closer. One day Katherine came to therapy ready to burst with excitement. "I figured out what to do! I am going to the Korean market and my mom agreed to help me learn how to make some Korean food dishes." Katherine was so proud of her idea and believed that food would be the ingredient to help connect her. "Food brings people together!"

Several weeks later Katherine came to therapy and reported that her strategy worked. "I shared the food I made and they began to talk to me! Of course, the adoption question came up rather quickly, but I was prepared, thanks to our previous talks about how to tell my story." Katherine slowly was accepted into the group. Eventually the other girls invited her into their homes and taught her more about her birth culture, customs, and language. Katherine's sense of self-worth soared. She spoke of feeling more complete as a person and was grateful for the opportunities her new friendships gave her. Therapy provided the safe place for her to share her struggles as she formulated who she was and what it meant to be Korean. Katherine's mother was able to recognize her limitations as far as giving Katherine what she needed in this area of identity integration and reached to therapy as a way to sort out such complex issues.

● ●

PERMANENCE

Permanence and its underlying issues of loss are also stuck spots for adopted adolescents. Adopted children are at risk for developing maladaptive beliefs about the security of the relationship with their parents. They think, *I've lost one set of parents; I could lose another.* This is especially true for those who have experienced multiple moves prior to adoption. Some adopted children go to great lengths to test their parents' commitment to them, sometimes without awareness of their own motivation. Therapy helps children understand how their behaviors reflect their sense of insecurity. Children need affirmation that their adoptive family can be a family forever.

Here are some thoughts teens commonly have about this issue:
- If my birth parents gave me away it could happen again.
- I have lived in so many homes, I am sure I will move again. Nothing lasts forever.
- When I go to college, will my parents be there for me?

Therapists who work with adopted adolescents sometimes get calls from distraught parents who are in a state of shock after finding out that their adolescent is failing a subject or two during the second semester of their senior year. The parent is often approached by the teen's school counselor who seems just as confused about why this is happening, when historically the adolescent has been an above-average student.

● ●

CASE EXAMPLE

Emily, age seventeen, was referred for counseling during the third quarter of her senior year when she began to skip school and fail to do her work. Emily had received early admission acceptance to a local state college, so her parents were surprised and alarmed by their daughter's sudden poor performance. During the initial session with Emily and her parents, the parents stated that the problem was getting even worse since referral. The parents had been notified recently by the school that Emily was in danger of failing the twelfth grade due to so many absences. Emily presented with a very flat affect and minimized the seriousness of the situation. "I can get it together, don't worry,

I'll pass," she said. She seemed unconcerned about the situation and complained that her parents were just making too big of a deal of the whole thing.

The parents mentioned in the initial session that Emily had a history of struggling with life transitions and sometimes became very depressed and dependent on her parents when her routine took new paths. This had occurred during transition from elementary school and again from middle school. These periods were quite tumultuous. Although this was a similar reaction, the parents were anxious because there was much more at stake.

During individual sessions with Emily, the therapist learned that the parents had told her that as soon as she went to college, they planned to sell their house and move to a retirement home at the beach. Exploring Emily's feelings about this led to tears. Emily said she could not tolerate the fact that the home she grew up in her whole life would disappear along with all her belongings, her room, and, most importantly, her parents!

"I feel I am losing everything; don't they know how hard this is for me?" she asked. In fact, Emily's parents had not realized how strongly their plans would affect their daughter. They thought she would be happy that they could move on with their dreams of retirement and she was moving on appropriately with her life plans. They never imagined that Emily would construe this as abandonment and that it would rekindle tremendous loss issues for her.

Emily and the therapist explored together her terrified feelings of losing yet another set of parents. The therapist helped her to understand the vulnerabilities connected with "separation." It was critical to help Emily express her fears and anxieties to her parents so they could affirm to Emily that they were not abandoning her. It was also important to educate and normalize this reaction for everyone. Emily was not overreacting. In fact, her reactions were quite appropriate given her life experiences. With help from her therapist and parents, she was able to separate the past from the future and look forward to her new challenges.

●●●●●●●●●●●●●●●●●●●●●●●●●

Unfortunately, the key is not always so easy to find or so easy to remedy. Any perceived or real vulnerability or deficiency in the adolescent may cause unusual anxiety about separation and emancipation. On the other hand, parental anxieties may lead either to clinging behavior with obstacles to emancipation or, conversely, to subtle messages of rejection. Either extreme can cause the adolescent to regress and fail in this final step of adolescence.

It is incumbent on the therapist to maintain an exploratory attitude that searches for comprehension and problem solving. One must avoid judgmental or critical attitudes toward parent or child. The therapist should maintain a quiet confidence that eventually a happy and triumphant emancipation will lead to an even warmer love and respectful friendship between parents and their adopted young adult.

Because our work with adopted children continually was revolving around loss issues, we sought a clinical framework with which to conceptualize loss in adoption. Following a cursory review of literature about loss, we discovered a book written by Pauline Boss, *Ambiguous Loss* (1999). Although Dr. Boss only briefly mentioned adoption in her book, her framework was applicable to adoption. In her book, Dr. Boss speaks of two kinds of ambiguous losses: In the first type of loss, the individual is physically present but psychologically absent, and in the other type, the individual is psychologically present and physically absent. Both of these definitions fit the losses inherent in adoption.

If children are taken from the custody of their birth families by social welfare officials, they are removed primarily due to neglect and or abuse issues. Although the children's birth parents were physically present, they were psychologically absent; they were unable to care for the physical, emotional, intellectual, and spiritual needs of their child. In other situations, the birth parents made a personal decision to place the child for adoption. No matter the reason for the relinquishment, as the child's comprehension of their adoption experience broadens, their birth parents become more "psychologically present" in their minds even though they remain physically absent. This does not pertain to cases in which the adoption is open. (We discuss that situation more fully in chapter 4.)

● ●

CASE EXAMPLE

Kayley, age fourteen, entered therapy following bouts of depression, lying, stealing, suicidal gestures, and family conflicts. Following a year of therapy, which included individual and group sessions, Kayley reluctantly acknowledged that she was indeed fearful of people leaving her, so she had constructed an elaborate defensive strategy to ensure that few individuals would be able to get close to her. She went on to describe the many masks she wore to elude people and protect herself. The therapist asked Kayley to draw every mask she wore and what purpose it served to protect her. Kayley approached the task with deliberation but guardedness. The process of revealing the mask was her first step in trusting someone — the first step in letting go of the fear of being hurt that led her to distance herself from others to ensure her self-preservation. "One of the masks I wore the most was my 'protective mask,' the one that was like a camouflage. I did not want people to know who I was. I was afraid of getting hurt. If someone doesn't know you, you can't get hurt."

Patience and perseverance are crucial in this work. Remember that Kayley had been in therapy for over a year with the same therapist before Kayley was able to confide her deep sorrows surrounding early abuse by her birth father. She finally shouted, "I was hurt. He hurt me. I am not going to let that happen to me again. Not ever!" Hiding behind the masks was the safety net that Kayley had constructed for herself as a protection from future pain and loss.

● ●

It is our task as therapists to supply the support and the skillfully applied pressure that will lead the adolescent to undertake and complete the painful task of unmasking themselves. Only by directly confronting and grieving the losses of relinquishment can adolescents free themselves from the past and be able to love fully and fearlessly in the present and future.

This grief work is not a static event. It ebbs and flows as the individual develops, and the losses take on different meaning at each key developmental stage. As the teen's understanding of adoption evolves, the grief associated with the loss will take on new meanings. In a recent therapy session, Kayley told her therapist, "I used to think if I hid behind my masks and didn't let people get close to me, I would protect myself from hurt. No one would leave me again. I learned that that is not true 'cause if you don't let people get close, you will always be alone. Loneliness is worse than the thinking about getting hurt."

Kayley has grown tremendously over the past few years. She rarely feels the need to hide behind the masks and has opened herself up to experiencing genuine relationships with her family and peers. Kayley can and does speak about her feelings regarding her past hurt and losses, but she is no longer paralyzed by them and feels safe enough now to risk hurt. She sees the benefit of allowing herself to let others get close to her.

IDENTITY

Two questions pose particular challenges for adopted children: Who am I and where did I come from? Not only must adopted adolescents think about how they are similar to and different from their adoptive parents, they must also think about how they are similar and different from their birth parents. Therapy supports the adolescent in the integration of a cohesive self. Many adopted adolescents ask themselves questions like these:

- Who am I? Am I like my adoptive parents or my birth parents or both?
- I know little about my birth parents, so how can I possibly figure out who I am?
- What does it mean that I am Hispanic? Korean? African-American?
- Who would I have been if I stayed with my birth family?
- Would life be different?
- What would be different about me?

For a moment, imagine what it must be like to not know anything about the people who brought you into the world. You do not know what they looked like, where they came from, or what their lives were like. You have no idea what their personalities were like, or their moods, temperament, intellectual capacities, strengths, or weaknesses. How would you relate, connect to, and identify with the parents who gave you your life and your genetic makeup without the answers to these powerful questions? How can you decide how you may be different from people you don't even know?

The overwhelming vastness of these unanswered questions is often the swirling internal void that leads the adopted adolescent to therapy. During a group therapy session for teens, Ann, age sixteen, adopted domestically at birth, responded to an assignment to describe through a drawing or writing how it feels to be adopted. Ann's writing clearly depicts her complex and varied feelings connected to her adoption experience. She speaks to the ambivalence surrounding her adoption and the questions about what life would have been like if she had not been relinquished.

How i feel about being adopted
BY ANN

I really do not know how I feel
I know I am confused at times
Sometimes it hurts when I think of how
Things could have been for me
Maybe things would have been different if my birth mother
Did not give me up
At times I imagine that if I were with her
Things would be better for me
Right now I don't enjoy being adopted
Why, I do not know
I am basically very confused and don't know who I am
Everyone has a goal in life and mine is to find my mother
And confront her

A major task of the adolescent period is to form an identity. Our identity is molded gradually from our values, beliefs, capabilities, talents, intellectual capabilities, sexual self-image, racial and ethnic heritage, personal goals and expectations, and, of course, our physical characteristics. All teens develop an awareness of these elements of self by determining how they are similar to their families and how they are different from them. These self-assessments are also strongly influenced by the youngster's perception of the parents' view of him or her.

As they age and mature, they are also influenced by identification figures in their wider world and by the evaluations that others place on them. During the adolescent period, peers gradually assume increasing importance in this process, but this does not alter the fact that the identity core evolves from the family. You can see that the quest to define self is a challenge for adoptees, who must determine who they are without the basic knowledge of where they came from or what their birth parents thought of them.

As we have discussed, adopted children naturally assume that the birth parents did not have a high opinion of their children, and they demonstrated that by giving their children away. Teens raised by their biological parents have the information about how they are similar to and different from their parents, and it is still a puzzling and often upsetting process. The task facing adopted adolescents is far more complex. They must figure out how they are like and different from *two* sets of parents, even though they may have limited or no knowledge of one set — the set that gave them their genetic heritage.

This somewhat shadowy set of parents may be the source of confusing fantasy and imagined characteristics that can really distort identity formation. The existence of the birth parents may also color and distort the youngster's perceptions of the adoptive parents.

How does the adopted adolescent accomplish this critical developmental milestone in the absence of information about their birth family? The normal search for self is compromised by the loss of the birth parents and complicated by the need to integrate the heritage of the birth family and the influences of the adoptive family. All of this while trying to gain a reasonably objective view of one's own strengths, weaknesses, and preferences — not to mention simultaneously adjusting to all the physical and mental changes inherent in the adolescent maturation. For adopted adolescents, it's no easy process.

Beneath the Mask

CASE EXAMPLE

Becca, a creative, engaging fifteen year old, entered therapy after symptoms of school phobia, peer conflicts, and self-destructive behaviors, all leading to severe family conflicts. Becca perceived the world around her as ungiving and rejecting of who she was. Week after week, Becca would come to therapy complaining about peers and adults who she said did not accept her. She felt that everyone misunderstood her actions and beliefs. These opinions led to difficulty maintaining relationships within her family and outside in her social arena. Becca felt rejected by most of her peers. She said her friendships seemed to be predicated on what she could give her peers in money or gifts rather than who she was as a person. Becca often wept and despaired that she couldn't figure out who she was without knowing who her birth parents were.

She repeated again and again, "I need to know who they were. I want to find out who I am." She wanted information about her birth history and requested that the therapist speak with her parents about getting this information. Becca's parents were ambivalent at first as they feared that, given all of Becca's problems, she would overidentify with the birth parents or that maybe some of the information would be difficult for Becca to accept and process. In their own therapy, Becca's parents were able to explore their fear and acknowledged they were afraid their daughter might want to search for her birth parents.

The therapist asked Becca's parents to walk in her shoes and to imagine what it must be like to try to figure out who you are without information about where you came from. The therapist helped them to remember the power of the stories and information they had growing up and how this history enabled them to build a secure sense of who they are now. Once they worked through their own fears and loss issues, they were able to see the importance of this quest.

Becca had been placed by a local agency. The parents contacted the agency and requested nonidentifying information regarding the birth parents. The agency social worker shared the information they held, including pre-placement history and a wealth of nonidentifying information, such as hair color and eye color of parents, and their weight, height, and body type. Becca's parents decided to utilize a therapy session as a forum to reveal this information with their daughter. They were uncomfortable presenting this information without therapeutic support because of their own fears, ambivalence toward the birth parents, and their daughter's fragile psyche.

The session was extremely constructive for all parties involved. In a very respectful, supportive process, Becca's parents communicated the information given to them by the agency social worker. Becca listened intently to each and every word her parents spoke. It was probably the only time in the sessions when she did not feel the need to challenge her parents' spoken word. Becca's parents could see what a freeing experience this was for Becca. It allowed her to lay aside so many misconceptions about her placement and genetic connections. Becca did not want to pursue an active search; she just wanted information to help her understand herself. Her parents provided her with a gift, the gift being knowledge about her story that proved to be emotionally liberating. (Becca speaks about this experience in more detail in chapter 5.)

Several weeks later Becca came into therapy, sat on the couch, stuck her face out, and opened her eyes wide, staring at the therapist. The therapist looked carefully at Becca, unsure about what Becca wanted her to notice. After all, Becca regularly presented herself in a variety of unique outfits, including gothic clothing and Renaissance outfits, and at times she had changed her hair color as well. The therapist was having difficulty picking up on what Becca was challenging her to discover.

Finally, Becca said, "You don't get it, just like my mom." The therapist asked Becca to tell her what was obviously being missed, but Becca just kept staring wide-eyed. Finally, as the therapist looked very closely, she could see that Becca's blue eyes had turned to brown. Becca had purchased cosmetic colored lenses, identifying with the information shared with her several weeks earlier that her birth mother had brown eyes.

Becca communicated her frustration that her mother had not noticed the change, and when Becca pointed it out to her, her mother minimized its significance. Struggling for sense of self, Becca was desperately seeking information to help her with the task. She was putting pieces together to create herself and looking for affirmation from her mom that this was a permitted and important task. She wanted to know that it was all right for her to be thinking about her birth parents and that they would not perceive her as disloyal.

Becca's dramatic behavior reflected her strong desire to communicate her internal turmoil as she searched for a solid sense of self yet felt conflicted by fears of disloyalty toward her parents. This is a time when, consciously or unconsciously, adoptees assess their biological and psychological bonds and attempt to achieve an identity that is some combination of both. By wearing brown contact lenses, Becca was reaching to find a symbolic fusion, putting the two pieces together to form one "me."

● ●

As adoptees move through adolescence, the quest for identity intensifies. Sometimes the quest is so powerful that it pulls adolescents to ponder a search beyond the intrapsychic journey they have embarked on. It is not surprising that adolescence is a time when heightened desire to search for birth parents surfaces. Initially, the teen may conduct an intrapsychic search, pondering the vast ramifications of such a quest. Their personal mission takes them on a tumultuous trek, encountering fears that their adoptive parents might be hurt by this desire. They also fear their own emotional reactions to the thought of opening their adoption and the uncertainty it may bring as they embark on this journey.

● ●

CASE EXAMPLE

Shantel, a fifteen-year-old adoptee, shares her story here. "Ever since I was a little girl, I did not know who my real father was. One day my mom told me that my stepdad was not my real dad. I eventually was taken away from my mom and put into foster care. People would say in front of me that my birth mom and I did not look anything alike. They told me I probably looked like my dad. But I didn't know who my dad was. In third grade when I had a visit with my mom, I asked her who my dad was. She told me it was one of two men. The first man was Caucasian. I knew he wasn't my dad because I did not look Caucasian.

"On the first mask I made in therapy, there are a lot of different colors on my face. I did not know who I was. This past year I found out that I am biracial. I am Hispanic and Caucasian. There was this big tribal meeting with my birth mom, adoptive parents, and therapist. Many questions were asked and things revealed.

"I asked my birth mom if she really did not know who my birth dad was to at least tell me something about him so I could know something about myself. I felt like a little kid putting a puzzle together without all the pieces. She finally then told me that my birth father was from Guatemala.

"The new mask is me! No questions asked. Nothing more to wonder about."

(Shante's masks appear in appendix A, figure 4.3 and figure 4.4.)

● ●

Although adoption literature in the past has indicated that teens only attempt information gathering at this stage, our experience at C.A.S.E. reflects a growing shift that teens want to go beyond gathering nonidentifying information to actually meeting their birth parents.

● ●

CASE EXAMPLE

Ariel was adopted domestically at birth. Over the years Ariel's curiosity about her origins increased. When she was eleven, she began having significant problems at home and resorted to solving her problems by running away. Eventually, as her problems worsened, her parents and helping professionals recommended she be hospitalized. While in treatment, Ariel continued to insist that her parents locate her birth family. She wanted to know her background, where she came from, the people with whom she was connected early in life. The therapist realized the need to help the adolescent and the family to accept the legitimacy of the quest.

"If we had to do it again," shared Ariel's mother in a recent phone interview, "my husband and I would do it exactly in the same way. We were struggling with how to help our daughter with all the problems she had and we were willing to do anything we could. During Ariel's sixth grade year she was having many difficulties, socially, academically, and emotionally. My husband and I were very active in trying to find the best answers for Ariel, to help her through this rocky road. As most parents would do, we took the usual steps, psychological testing, finding the right doctors, therapists, and even changing schools.

"During one especially rough evening, my husband and I had a realization. Even though through the years we gave her tidbits about her birth family we suddenly came to the conclusion that we had to give her more. Although Ariel was adopted privately, we had met and spoken to her birth mom a number of times. We did not know how anyone in her birth family would feel about being contacted twelve years after she was adopted. Our daughter made us realize that one of the major issues was that she wanted to know more about who she was and where she came from. In our situation, opening Ariel's adoption gave her a special connection with her identity that she craved so much. From the minute we gave her her brother's picture and address, we knew in our hearts it was the right thing to do. Because of this decision, Ariel and our family have added more love and family members to our lives. Many people have said to us 'How could you have taken that chance?' We never looked at it that way. However, I would advise that any family who proceeds with opening an adoption should take the steps to work with an adoption therapist. There are so many issues for the child to juggle after a reunion. Once you make the decisions to open an adoption, it's open forever."

Ariel's search began at age eleven when she received a letter from her maternal grandmother that included a picture of her older biological brother along with his address. In revisiting that experience, Ariel said, "The picture changed my life. Ever since I was little I wanted to meet my birth mom, and my mom would always say, 'Someday, Ariel.' Now the someday arrived! I was so excited that I immediately wrote my brother a letter."

Dear Mike,

Hi, how are you? I'm your sister Ariel. I am eleven years old and live in Maryland. What kind of music do you like? I like rock bands like Greenday, Orgy, some Manson. What grade are you in? Do you like any sports? How tall are you? When is your birthday? Mine is January 10, 1986. What are some things you like to do? I like to talk on the phone, draw, swim and listen to music. What's your biggest hobby?

The reason I am writing you is because my parents showed me a picture of you. I was like WOW, I have an older brother. I also have a younger brother, his name is Matthew. My mom's name is Ellen and my dad's name is Al. I hope to hear from you soon. Always your lil sis — Ariel

Not too long after her letter, she received the following letter:

Dear Ariel,

Hello back, I am your brother Michael. When I got your letter I was like oh my gosh this is my sister and I could not help from crying. I am so happy to hear from you. I like Boyz to Men, Greenday and stuff like that. I am in the 10th grade and I am 5'9". I like football; basketball and I play the drums. I am sending you a picture of my best buddies and me. Well it is getting late and I have to go to bed. Lots of love from your bro — Michael

With the support of her parents and her maternal grandmother, at the age of twelve, Ariel met her biological brother, maternal grandmother, maternal grandfather, and extended family. Ariel's birth mother remained estranged from her family and was not able to be located at the initial search. When asked what her search has given her, Ariel responded with clarity, "It gave me my background — my extended family. It gave me the stories of my family — of things that happened in the past to my birth family; it gave me a sense of what they were like. It gave me my brother! I could relate to the stories and find a way to then make them my own memories."

For Ariel it also gave her a powerful genetic connection. During one of her therapy sessions she reflected on the first meal she shared with her brother. "I couldn't believe how much we were alike. We ordered the same thing. We ate the same way — first we both ate half of the burger, then half our French fries, then the rest of the burger, and then we would polish off the fries! The weirdest thing, though, was that we both held our forks in the same way. Also I noticed that we both stand on the side of our feet when we are nervous."

Ariel reveled in this awareness and said, "For the first time I felt a connection with someone on this level." When asked what she meant about "this level," Ariel said, "You know, someone who is connected to me biologically. I finally could share in knowing what it's like when someone says 'you're just like your brother'... what that really feels like. Not until I met my brother did I have such a powerful connection with anyone in my life!"

The parties involved in such reunions usually hold intricate expectations, and the outcomes are often powerful. "I really believed in my heart that everything was going to be perfect. It would be like saying hello to an old family member. I thought that when I met them, it would change me. I thought it would make me less angry, and all my problems would go away. Instead at first it was awkward. We were not old family members — we were strangers really. I wanted to hug my brother, but I held back because I did not know if it would be okay. My problems didn't go away; instead they actually doubled! Now that I had opened these relationships, I had to figure out how to maintain them — so much has happened in the past. It is really hard to explain — it's like starting a video in the middle of the story."

When asked what drawbacks she experienced, Ariel cited geography as the primary barrier to maintaining this connection. Unfortunately, her birth family resides on the opposite side of the country. And she said, "We were raised so differently. I grew up in a suburban, middle-class neighborhood, raised Jewish, and Michael, my brother, grew up in a rural area near the water and was raised Christian."

Looking back upon this unfinished journey, Ariel had no regrets about searching for her birth family. She continues to struggle with not being able to meet her birth mother. Ariel has learned a great deal about her birth mother from her grandmother and brother. "The information they told me is bad stuff," she said. "I wish it were good, but it's not."

Over a year ago, Ariel, age seventeen, approached her therapist about the possibility of contacting her birth mother. She had received information from her grandmother that her birth mother had resurfaced. Much dialogue occurred between Ariel and the therapist, and later her parents were included. Ariel wanted to learn more about her birth mom from her birth mom herself, not information filtered through the lenses of her extended family. Furthermore, as her issues regarding identity and sexuality were deepening, she pondered the existence of her birth father. Who was he? Did her birth mom have information about him?

Ariel's parents, while supportive of the reunion, feared negative outcomes of her contacting her birth mother because her birth mother had been unreliable and had difficulty maintaining relationships with her family. The therapist had to consider and explore the parents' reactions to the search and also inquire about any additional information they might have that was not yet shared with their child that might have a bearing on the process.

● ●

It is just as important for the therapist to carefully assess the adolescent's emotional readiness and to explore slowly and respectfully the dynamics behind the desire for the contact.

What is the adolescent hoping to find? Are his expectations realistic? What questions does she wish to pose? What does he dream this reunion will be like? What might she actually find? These questions may seem overwhelming and one might doubt the adolescent's capability to handle the search, but our experience has been that when an adolescent and his or her family is engaged in a strong, therapeutic relationship with a clinician who understands adoption issues, the journey can be embarked upon.

It is important to keep in mind that the adoptive parents need help through this process too. The increased interest in birth parents often stimulates underlying fears that have been dormant for some time within the minds of adoptive parents. Adopted adolescents, in their search for self, reactivate in the adoptive parents the powerful realization that the birth parents do exist. It may be difficult for them to accept that these distant relations are an integral part of who their children are and will become. This can pose many difficulties for the adoptive family, particularly because the adolescent may begin to challenge their parental status as a normal part of development.

● ●

CASE EXAMPLE

Justin, a fifteen-year-old, was always difficult in family sessions. On this particular day he began belittling his mother in a family therapy session. She was too old. She lacked spontaneity. She wore funky clothes. She yelled too much. He seemed to be purposely trying to hurt and reject his mother.

The therapist acknowledged the things he didn't like about his mother but wondered what things about her Justin *did* like. Justin looked at the therapist as if she had three heads and said, "Nothing." The therapist then asked

Justin to describe the ways in which he and his mother were similar. Justin exploded, "We have nothing in common! How could we when we are not connected by blood?" Needless to say, his mother was distraught.

The therapist accepted his comments but talked with him calmly about the fact that we can share similarities with people who have no genetic connection with us. As an example, the therapist pointed out that many couples that live together for a long time report that they become very much alike. This pause and support allowed the mother to regain her composure. She began to describe examples of how she felt Justin was like his father and her. Justin was guardedly attentive at first but eventually began to nod at the accuracy of some of his mother's observations.

In a follow-up session with the mother, she said that she had been stunned at Justin's sense of disconnection from his parents. She explained that they had often pointed out his similarities to them throughout his earlier childhood. She hadn't realized how important it was to reinforce this strongly once he reached adolescence. She was able to gain insight into her son's challenge in formulating a solid sense of self and the need for her participation in helping him connect all the pieces together.

● ● ● ● ● ● ● ● ● ● ● ● ● ● ● ● ● ● ● ●

This is a crucial issue in working with adopted teens as they ponder who they are and how they are similar to and different from their parents. In biological families, similarities and differences are typically discussed more readily. Therapists working with adopted adolescents will want to explore with teens how they see themselves in relation to both sets of parents. Following this exploration, the therapist may want to consider inviting the parents to join the process.

We have found asking the parents to tell their teen how they see the similarities between themselves and their child to be an invaluable tool. Teens are often amazed by their parents' perceptions and feel a stronger sense of bonding and claiming by their parents.

LOYALTY

The issue of loyalty is a common stuck spot for adopted adolescents. Many such teens experience guilt related to their frequent and intense thoughts and feelings about their birth parents. Fearing the disapproval of their parents, adopted teens may hide their feelings and struggle alone with their emotional connection to their birth parents and the questions they have about them. Therapy must help to remove the teens' guilt and normalize the feelings that they may hold for their birth parents. Thinking about birth parents does not mean adolescents love their parents any less.

Here are some typical thoughts of adopted teens:

- I have so many questions about my birth parents; but if I ask my parents, will they get upset?

- I know things were bad at home when I was a baby, but I wonder about my mom and grandmother. Maybe I will live with them again someday, so how can I really feel like my adoptive parents are my family?

- I think about my sister who was not adopted. I love her so much.

Twelve years ago, the Center for Adoption Support and Education was awarded a demonstration project funded by the federal government's Department of Health and Human Services to develop a loss and grief model for children to help them resolve early trauma and loss issues so that they would be able to successfully attach to their new family. The services were to be delivered to foster care children ages ten to eighteen in the public child welfare system. The concurrent planning process is a two-pronged approach that involves working toward family reunification and, at the same time, establishing an alternative plan for adoption if reunification proves to be impossible.

The research design and evaluation was conducted by a team from the Department of Family Science at the University of Maryland, College Park. The evaluation was based on a time services analysis of responses of children and their foster parents to a battery of assessment instruments, which were administered in three- and six-month intervals. The research design included a tool, the Psychological Presence Measure (Fravel and Kohler, 2001), a thirteen-item measure grounded in Boss's (1999) theory of ambiguous loss that assesses the child's psychological attachment to their birth parents and ascertains the children's loyalty and emotional connections to their birth families (Kohler et al., 2001). Like many children in U.S. foster care systems, these children had spent their early years of life with their birth families.

One of the most important contributions to come out of this study was the validation of the children's loyalty issues and emotional connections to their birth families. Of the seventy-four children participating in the project, 91.3 percent said at baseline that they still felt their birth mother in their mind or heart (psychological presence) and 63.4 percent said the same of their birth father. The reality was that the children, both males and females, were thinking about their birth parents frequently and intensely. In fact, 56 percent of the youngsters reported feeling their birth mother "in their heart or mind" daily. Forty percent of the children felt their birth father "in their heart or mind" daily.

The children were more likely to feel their birth mother's presence on their birthday, on Mothers' Day, on the day they entered foster care, and other holidays. Birth fathers were thought of on Fathers' Day, the child's birthday, and during religious events. The

Beneath the Mask

vast majority of the children, more than 85 percent, felt that their birth mother was still a part of their family, and a substantial majority — almost 69 percent of them — felt that their birth father was still a part of the family.

It is important to note that the children's scores showed very little change between baseline and follow-up, suggesting that the children's psychological attachment to their birth parents is deeply rooted and that their feelings do not simply go away over time.

The findings regarding the powerful presence of birth parents for foster children may be one of the most important contributions of that study. One may conclude that for children in foster care, their biological parents are still very much present in a psychological sense. Parental psychological presence may serve a protective psychological purpose, keeping the children psychologically attached to parents even when physical attachments are being disrupted.

Our clinical experience brings us to conclude that *all* adopted children ponder the existence and character of their birth parents at some time in their lives. At C.A.S.E., children report again and again that they daydream about their birth parents, fantasize about them, and often pine for them. It does not matter what the adoptive experience was. Children who were placed at birth, children placed later in life, children placed domestically, and those placed internationally, all spend a lot of energy and time working mentally on this issue.

● ●

CASE EXAMPLE

Juanita, a twelve-year-old, and her prospective adoptive parent were referred to C.A.S.E. so that we could help to prepare her for adoption. Following three months of conjoint sessions with the mother and Juanita as well as individual sessions with the teen, the prospective mother called the clinician. She said that she had to make Juanita stop talking about her birth mother. She felt that it was interfering with her ability to connect with her. The mother said emphatically, "Juanita needs to move on!"

The clinician knew there was no way to get Juanita to stop talking about her birth mother and, of course, knew that she should not stop. Still the mother's feelings had to be respected while she was led to see what Juanita was struggling with. Fortunately, at the initial assessment, the therapist had learned that the prospective adoptive mother had lost her own mother nineteen months earlier. Taking a huge risk, the clinician asked the mother how she would feel if her friends told her that they were sick and tired of her talking about her mother. What if her friends pointed out that her mother has been dead for over a year and a half and that it is time for her to move on and just get over it? Since her mother is dead she should just forget her.

The mother started to cry, realizing how selfish she had been. In her heart she knew very well that Juanita needed to remember her mother. The therapist was able to help the mother permit the teen to embrace her birth mother within her heart and at the same time open her heart to let her new mom in.

● ● ● ● ● ● ● ● ● ● ● ● ● ● ● ● ● ● ● ●

Parents and professionals need to accept that the psychological presence of birth parents is real and alive in the minds of their teens. We need to accept the depth of these thoughts and the difficulty teen adoptees may have in sharing them. "I am so afraid to tell my mom that I think about my birth mom," said Amy, a sixteen-year-old

Beneath the Mask

adolescent. "I know it will hurt her. In the past when I mentioned my thoughts to her, she acted upset. I love her and don't want to hurt her."

The frequency and intensity of these thoughts may vary, depending on the adolescent's personal adoption story, but the psychological presence of their birth families does not. This intense mental activity is depicted powerfully in a poem written by Elyse, a thirteen-year-old girl who was referred to our center following a hospitalization due to suicidal ideations. The poetry was found by her mother during her hospitalization. Elyse had been e-mailing the poem to friends.

untitled
BY Elyse

You are always in my heart
You are always in my thoughts
You are always on my mind
Everyday and every time

Not a day goes by that I don't think of you
And how my life would be like if I had lived with you

You are always in my spirit
You are always in my life
You are always with me
And I could not ever forget you.

This adolescent has never met her birth mother. She was placed at birth and has had no contact with her birth mother. Elyse began writing about her birth mother as her thoughts about her adoption became more prominent in her life and the feelings connected to her abandonment became more powerful. She never communicated her thoughts about her birth mother to her parents. The fear of upsetting her parents prevailed.

Too often we are asked by child welfare workers, prospective parents, and even adoptive parents to suggest ways they can help children to forget their birth connections. Especially with older placements, both professionals and parents sometimes believe that the child's feelings and thoughts about their birth parents or foster parents will impede the attachment and bonding process to the new family.

● ● ● ● ● ● ● ● ● ● ● ● ● ● ● ● ● ● ● ●

CASE EXAMPLE

Luba, age fifteen, had come to America three years before with her biological sister, Irina, age sixteen. Her composition depicts again the depth of the adopted child's connections to birth families and the weight of their losses upon them. Luba and Irina left behind an older birth sister, Olga, age twenty-one. Recently in therapy, Luba shared her profound grief surrounding the separation from Olga. Luba recently has been having deepening thoughts about her sister. She's been agonizing over her ambivalence toward her life here and the worry and sadness she carries in not being able to see her sister. Luba wrote:

MISS YOU

Not for long I saw
My dear sister Olga.
But for long I have prayed
To see her soon again.

I have struggled through
When the tears came down.

Beneath the Mask

And it almost seemed
As if the world stopped spinning around

For a long time I thought
I would never see her again
With her wonderful daughter
Who gives her hope everyday

As I pray till this day
I still hope to say
And to run to her

When that one day
Comes to me I'll say
That I have missed you still
Until this day

● ● ● ● ● ● ● ● ● ● ● ● ● ● ● ● ● ● ● ●

Joining this journey with the adopted adolescent is both complex and challenging. At times it can be daunting. It requires a deep understanding of the inherent developmental tasks of adoption and how teens can become burdened by the complexities of the emotional significance of their adoption experience. However, it is a journey that can be embarked upon with the adolescent, leading them to self-awareness, healing, and growth.

We believed what we read in adoption books and what we saw in the movies — that love conquers all when you're raising a child. Not always the case we learned.
Adoptive Dad

parental stuck spots

Helping Adoptive parents over the Hurdles

Adolescence raises many questions for parents whose children are adopted. They ponder the fact that their child may struggle with identity issues as they grapple with the notion of having two sets of parents. They fear their child's sense of safety, security, and stability will somehow be undermined by growing trepidation surrounding the circumstances of their relinquishment. Many of the adoptive families we treat seem to be aware that being adopted will make the normal challenges of adolescence even harder for their teen. The issues are complex and have many layers of underpinnings. Helping parents to understand the interplay between normal adolescent adjustment issues and adoption issues is the hallmark of therapy when working with adopted teens and their families.

There have been few case reports depicting the psychoanalytic understanding of adoptive parents (Brodzinsky and Schechter, 1990). Brief discussions in the adoption literature suggest that some adoptive parents will struggle with intrapsychic conflicts such as infertility, parent-child bonding, and their right to take total parental ownership and authority with their adopted child. Parents also grapple with trying to understand the child's emotional response to the adoption experience and the youngster's reworking of the separation and individuation processes that surface in adolescence (Brodzinsky and Schecter, 1990).

Parents most likely will be the referring source when an adolescent comes in for therapy. Typically they will reveal the presenting behaviors that have led them to seek help. For adoptive parents, the quest for help may be a little more complex, and therapists may find ambivalence about the role adoption may play in the clinical picture. Even though parents may indicate at the phone intake that adoption may be a factor in the problem, they often seem unsure about its significance. There seems to be a fear of putting too much weight in this area.

A SURVEY OF PARENTS

To gain a broader perspective on this issue for this book, we created a survey for parents who had sought clinical services for their children. We would like to share some of the survey's findings in hopes of heightening awareness of how adoption presents itself clinically from a parental perspective. The survey also covers factors that led to the parents' greater understanding of adoption issues and which elements of therapy increased their capacity to help their teen. We also asked which adoption issues turned out to play a significant role in the teen's life. Twenty-five parents returned their survey. Some were from husbands and wives who filled them out separately.

Regarding the primary concerns that led parents to seek treatment, the issues were varied. "My daughter had a history of self-injurious behaviors and threats of self harm, depression, lying, stealing. I believe my daughter was depressed surrounding early abandonment issues." Another family reported, "Our daughter was acting out violently and displayed mood swings which were out of control. She had boundary problems and did not understand proper interpersonal relationships. This all began six weeks after we brought her home from Russia. She was thirteen years old."

Another reported, "The primary reason we sought treatment for our twelve-year-old daughter was growing negative change in behavior. From the time we met her at two years old, she had mood swings and was not an easy child, but after puberty she became increasingly difficult."

Another parent said, "Our son had exhibited behavior management problems and our home lacked family peace. He engaged in all kinds of misbehavior: lying, stealing, breaking family rules, stealing from family members. He was very impulsive and had anger management problems."

Other parents reported self-image issues, anger problems, noncompliance, school difficulties, social isolation, drug use, inappropriate use of the Internet, and depression.

As you can see, there is some reference to adoption, but as a rule only in those situations in which the child was placed at an older age. Of all the parents surveyed, sixteen acknowledged that they had some suspicion that adoption issues might be a major factor in their teen's life, but they were surprised when therapy revealed the depth of such issues and how they were related to the presenting symptomatology. Nine parents were less assured. "I had for some time an inkling that adoption issues might be a part of the problem without any specific evidence," wrote one dad of a fifteen-year-old son.

THE CASE FOR INCLUDING PARENTS
When working with teens, the therapist may be tempted to forge ahead in a very autonomous relationship with the youngster, leaving the parents out unless the teen begins to engage in or will not stop engaging in high-risk behaviors. However, when working with adoptees, we have found it imperative to include the parents in the therapeutic relationship from the beginning.

A note of caution is important here. Sometimes therapists may be working with an adolescent who cannot tolerate sharing the clinician with his or her parents. If this is the case, it is recommended that the family be seen by another therapist who will do the family work. Both therapists should be able to work collaboratively and help to integrate adoption issues into the family work. At C.A.S.E., we disclose to the teen that the two therapists will be working closely and that we will help the teen identify those adoption issues that need to be addressed as a family.

In our clinical experience, adoption does play a significant role in the development and persistence of the symptoms that cause parents to seek counseling for their child in the first place. By engaging the parents, therapists can create a greater understanding of the adoption issues, a process that will ultimately enhance their capacity to support their teen. The treatment protocol is based on a psycho-educational model, teaching and reteaching the teen and the family about the emotional significance of the adoption experience and the differences that exist between an adoptive family and a biological family.

TREATMENT TECHNIQUES FOR PARENTS

Education

We wanted to glean from parents who were involved in their teen's therapy what factors actually led to their deeper understanding of adoption issues and what enabled them to increase their capacity to support their teen. Ninety-eight percent of the parents surveyed said that the therapist's explanation of how and why adoption is affecting their adolescent was the single most helpful element of therapy. The ability to engage in a psycho-educational didactic exchange with the teen and the family has proven a very effective treatment strategy for our families. By the time their children are teens, adoptive parents have typically put away the adoption books they purchased when they first adopted, and they usually lack the knowledge of the impact the adoption experience has in adolescence.

It becomes the therapist's job to educate the family about the normal developmental issues that are emerging in the life of a teen adoptee. As one mother described in her survey, "We participated in numerous family sessions with our daughter, which I believe were imperative for our family's healing. The ability to talk with a trained adoption professional who could provide insight and guidance to overcome the hurdles and move forward was invaluable. My daughter and I both worked hard to heal and are committed to living in a healthy, happy family. Our desire to make things work certainly played a role in our healing. However, the most important ingredient was our therapist. She understood teenagers, trauma, and most importantly adoption. She was able to help us understand, change, and grow into a healthier family."

Our experience reflects that adoptive parents are extremely open and receptive to the newly found knowledge and are eager to obtain more. It will be the therapists' responsibility to impart this information, so they will have to become familiar with the adoption literature and which books are good to recommend for parents and teens to read. (See appendix B for a bibliography for parents, teens, and younger children.)

Exploring Parental Emotions and Attitudes

Just as important as helping the parents understand how their teen is embracing adoption is giving parents the opportunity to increase their awareness of their own emotions and reactions to adoption. Typically at this developmental stage, the adoptive parent is thrust into a resurgence of unresolved loss issues embedded in years of infertility. They still may secretly be holding onto faint dreams of birth children. They may be experiencing anger, resentment, and guilt at being denied a child by birth, especially when their teen exhibits behaviors that are incongruent with their personal values, beliefs, and expectations. At that point, they may hear the echoes of family members and friends who warned them that there would be trouble trying to raise a child that is not theirs.

Communication

Interestingly, the results of the survey reflected how important it was to the parents that they had the opportunity to receive direct communication and input from their teen. In fact, all twenty-five individuals surveyed identified this as a critical factor that led to their greater understanding of adoption issues. Most therapists treating adolescents might be surprised that the teen would even tolerate having the parents present in therapy. We have found that the quest for adoption clarity engages the adolescent in dialogue with their parents. It is amazing to watch nonverbal, semiresistant teens engage in sessions once they are given permission to talk about those feelings and thoughts that have been percolating inside of them for months or maybe even years.

It often takes some individual therapeutic time with an adolescent before he or she can begin to delve into the delicate concerns of adoption with their parents. But when it happens, it is a powerful and moving process for all involved. As one parent stated, "Being involved in family therapy led to more openness about adoption and provided our family with the guidance to explore and try to begin to understand what our son was feeling. I can remember one session when our son was angry with us because he felt we minimized his feelings in regards to some pretty big adoption issues. Our therapist turned to me and asked me what I thought it felt like to walk in the shoes of an adopted person. I felt at that moment that all the air was knocked out of me. I was so taken by the question, or should I say struck by the fact, because, honestly, as an adoptive parent I had never once thought about what it would be like to be adopted. I mean I had read all the books but no one had ever posed the question to me in that way. I

Beneath the Mask

truly did not know what it felt like nor had I given my son the chance to ever really tell me. "

THE SIX STUCK SPOTS

At C.A.S.E., we approach therapeutic work with adoptive parents within the contextual framework of the six crucial issues that we discussed in the previous chapter — reason for adoption, missing information, differences, permanence, identity, and loyalty. Not only are these issues stuck spots for teens, they are the critical issues for parents. We examine them thoroughly here.

Reasons for Adoption

"I am leery about telling Sam the *whole* story. I do not want to upset him." These words were spoken by an adoptive mother who was struggling with her son's persistent question, "Why didn't my birth mother keep me?" Adoptive parents will tell you that one of the hardest challenges in adoptive parenting is explaining their child's adoption story.

While they begin with the best intentions in mind, they often stray off course when they have to reveal aspects of the story that may be difficult. It is no longer adequate to recapitulate the version of the adoption story that was given when the child was younger. This simplified version usually goes something like this: "Your birth mom could not take care of you, and Daddy and I so much wanted to be parents, and we adopted you."

By adolescence the quest for information deepens and the story must be revisited. It is in adolescence that potentially painful and complex information needs to be shared. As Joyce Maguire Pavao writes in *The Family of Adoption* (1998, 98), "The greatest gift we can give them is to tell them their truths and to help them make sense of these truths, especially when they are complicated and harsh."

In *Psychology of Adoption* (1990), Dr. David Brodzinsky points out that "human beings story their worlds." As adoption specialists, we work toward honoring the adoption story because it is central in the life of an adoptive family. Like children in birth families, adopted children want and need to know facts about their beginnings. They are hungry for information: How did I get here? Where was I born? Who was there? How long did it take until I was born? Was I healthy? Such questions are just a sample from the bottomless pool of curiosity.

In this developmental period almost all children seek to expand their understanding of their story. What separates birth families from adoptive families at this juncture is that the adoptive family often does not have all the pieces of the story. This leaves the children with the need to reconstruct their story like a detective. The adoptive parents may have only given them the bits of the adoption story that fit the parents' comfort level. During preadolescence they may add aspects about their story hinted at by brief comments or reactions by their adoptive parents and a little from their own creative imagination. By the time the youngster reaches adolescence the text is spotty and rather unreliable.

The aspect of the story that teens most commonly seek to expand and clarify is why they were relinquished. Unfortunately, it is this very piece of the story that most adoptive parents find most difficult to explain. In fact, adoptive parents often do not know the true reasons that led the birth parents to relinquish. Unless the adoptive parents had early communication with the birth parents, the *why* is often unknown. It is here that they may seek help from an adoption professional in charting and navigating these dangerous shoals. It is better to help the parents acknowledge to their teen that in fact they don't know and move toward a dialogue of speculation. Speculation is better than providing the adoptee with false information.

● ●

CASE EXAMPLE
"I always felt like I was born a mistake," said Becca sadly during an interview for this book. "I thought that if they — my

Beneath the Mask

birth parents — didn't want to keep me then I had to have been a mistake. I was not worthy to be here. My birth mom didn't want me, my birth dad didn't want me. Those words kept pounding my brain.

"Then something incredible happened to me. I pushed my parents in therapy to get me more information about my birth parents. My therapist helped me with this. My parents were really nervous about what I would find. We called the agency where I was adopted from and I found out that my birth mom tried to parent me for four months — she really *did care about me*!! She cared enough to try to keep me, the records said that she tried but eventfully found it was too hard by herself to raise me. For fourteen years I believed I was a mistake! Providing me with some of the missing information allowed me to no longer see myself as a kid that no one wanted!"

● ●

The exploration of the adoption story, which embraces the complicated question of why the child was placed for adoption, is an important tool in family therapy with adoptive parents. It can shed light on the level of communication within the family system about adoption and may also bring out underlying emotions related to unresolved feelings of loss and grief, loyalty issues, and secrecy. Family therapy uses the adoption story to help parents overcome the stumbling blocks related to their ability to openly communicate about adoption and creates a safe forum in which to explore the complexities of the relinquishment.

Missing Information
In chapter 4 we described the prevalence of the feeling that adoptees carry of being a part of a puzzle with a missing piece. Adolescents

need all the pieces of the puzzle to form a solid sense of self. It is no wonder that the adopted teenager pushes hard to find answers to their questions. They push hard because they must find the missing pieces of their puzzle!

Becca, whom we have met before, really gets on her soapbox on this topic. "There should be no closed adoptions allowed! It's not fair that I can't know where I came from, where certain traits are from, who I look like. How can people think this is good for us? Let them try to figure out who they are with no information. It's like running without legs — you simply can't do it."

As the windows of adoption are opened and communication between parent and child is nurtured and encouraged, the teen becomes more comfortable in seeking needed information. Helping parents to understand the importance of this quest for information is crucial. Yet one must tread cautiously at this juncture because the adoptive parents may be holding onto information they have never shared, believing the information to be difficult and potentially harmful to their child. The family belief system says that if this information sees the light of day it will lead to very destructive events. The therapist cannot charge recklessly ahead without dealing with the parental fears. Still, this must be done. As Pavao (1998) puts it, truth is a gift. Let us also remember Lifton's (1994, 65) eloquent statement, "If your personal narrative doesn't grow and develop with you, with concrete facts and information, you run the danger of becoming emotionally frozen. You cannot make the necessary connections between the past and the future that everyone needs to grow into a cohesive self."

● ● ● ● ● ● ● ● ● ● ● ● ● ● ● ● ● ● ● ●

CASE EXAMPLE
A mother of a seventeen-year-old male contacted our center requesting a consultation with an adoption specialist.

She was having some struggles with her son who was pushing her for information about his birth parents. She said that she needed some help sorting out the issue. Barbara, age fifty-two, presented as a very articulate, even-tempered person who was experiencing a heightened sense of anxiety as her son kept pushing her for more information about his birth father. Over the years he had been more interested in his birth mother and had never brought up his birth father until his senior year in high school. When asked why this was unsettling to her, she began to cry. She revealed that the birth father had a dependency on alcohol, had been physically abusive toward the birth mother, and abandoned both of them when her son was nine months old. Unable to make it on her own, the birth mom made an adoption plan.

Barbara told her son that she did not know anything about his birth father as she feared what impact this information would have upon him as he was growing up. "I worried that he would somehow identify with this man and think in some way he could grow up to be like him." Now that her son was "pushing" for more information, she felt badly that she had lied to him, but she didn't know how to tell him the truth. "If I tell him what I know, he will hate me for lying to him. I should have never hidden the truth from him. I know this now, but it may be too late."

Barbara engaged the help of the therapist to assist her and her son as they worked through this critical issue in their relationship. Barbara needed a great deal of understanding and acceptance of the reasons why she chose to handle the situation this way for so many years. She spoke of her isolation as a single mom and how being a single mom increased her fears that her son might overidentify with his birth father. She reasoned that since her son was being parented without a father, he might be especially vulnerable to that fantasy connection.

Once Barbara could sort out her own issues she was able to understand the importance of providing the answers to her son's questions as he moved thorough this challenging time in his life. With the help of the therapist, Barbara chose to bring her son Jason into therapy with her and slowly begin to share the remaining facts about his adoption story that she had fearfully hidden. Surprisingly to Barbara, Jason accepted the information and shared relief that he finally had some knowledge about his birth father even though he felt sad to hear about the poor choices his birth father had made. Jason shared that he had secretly believed that his birth father was dead since no one spoke of him. The new information opened the possibility that maybe one day he could meet his birth father.

● ●

Adoptive parents can experience a great deal of anxiety around the sharing of difficult information or the lack of birth family information. They deeply want to fill in the missing pieces for their children, but often don't know where to begin. Family therapy can explore realistic ways to obtain more information when possible and help to make decisions about opening up closed adoptions. Family therapy can support parents through the process of seeking information, decision making, and the possibility of connecting with birth family members.

Differences
When infertility issues have not adequately been explored and at least accepted, if not resolved, the adoptive parents often carry

tremendous expectations for their adopted children. They are very likely to project the fantasy of the birth child they imagine they would have had onto their adopted child. As the turmoil of adolescence erupts, the adoptive parents' sensitivity to differences becomes accentuated and at times creates a tremendous conflict in the parent-child relationship. The parents are often at least dimly aware of the source of their disappointment. They are often surprised and uncomfortable to recognize that at this late stage in the game they are still holding on to issues related to the loss of the birth child. They may feel tremendous guilt, recognizing that these perceived differences are opening doors that they thought were shut long ago.

● ●

CASE EXAMPLE

Yolanda, a soft-spoken woman came to our office for a consultation and within the first few seconds of the meeting began to cry. She had been in therapy for years as she has had difficulty bonding with her daughter, whom she adopted at birth following years of infertility treatments. "I have tried and tried to figure out my feelings but never seem to reach a personal level of understanding. My therapist just doesn't seem to understand this intense conflict I am struggling with.

"My daughter is nothing like me or my extended family. I was raised in a highly academic environment. Both my parents were professors who enjoyed reading, classical music, and family discussions. Our home was quiet and intellectually stimulating.

"Over the years my daughter has developed into the complete opposite of who I am and who her grandparents are. She is aggressive, athletic, spontaneous, extroverted, and very social. She has little interest in academics and likes loud rap music.

"My parents can't understand why I cannot control her. They think I have failed as a parent and should have steered her away from the things that she is interested in. Now that she is a teenager I have resigned myself that she will not change. The problem now is that my daughter is staying out late with friends, threatens to run away, and is disengaging from our family."

Yolanda agreed to bring her daughter Camille into therapy so we could get a sense as to how this family incongruence has affected her sense of identity as well as to ascertain the seriousness of her increased risk-taking behaviors. Camille presented as a tough, disenfranchised adolescent who certainly did not want any more helpful adults in her life. As sessions proceeded it became clear that Camille was painfully aware of the differences between her and her family.

"I have felt like an alien living in this house, with people who are alien to me. They don't like me because I am nothing like them. If I wear a size 8 shoe, it's impossible to try to fit into a 6. They want me to be a 6. I can never seem to please my parents, especially my mom! We are so different!" Camille began to cry and said she didn't understand why adoption was so great. "When you are taken from people who you are like and given to strangers who are not like you, it sucks!"

● ● ● ● ● ● ● ● ● ● ● ● ● ● ● ● ● ● ● ●

For Yolanda and Camille the journey was difficult and the prognosis for change was guarded. Slowly, Yolanda was able to begin to embrace her daughter's differences but she continued to be

beneath the mask

emotionally distant and apprehensive of intimacy with her daughter. Camille joined an adolescent group and found great support among her peers as she opened herself up to explore the disconnect between herself and her mother. Camille's plans for the future are to search for her birth family. "I want to find someone who is just like me," she says.

Adoptive parents who are parenting transracially or transculturally often find these differences to be heightened during adolescence. At this stage, teens are aligning themselves with a peer group, but during the adolescent period teens who are of different race than their parents are scrutinized by their peers more than ever before. Questions of where they choose to fit in and where they actually are accepted become significant challenges to the transracial adoptee.

Adoptive parents are often surprised to learn from their transracial teen that the world is not the wonderful embracing place they believed it to be. Differences are not necessarily celebrated and racism hasn't vanished. In fact, a large number of teens we have treated over the years have had very painful experiences with racism. These lead to thought-provoking and upsetting sessions with their parents as they recount the racism they encounter on a daily basis.

Unfortunately, racism crosses all boundaries and can be found in both public and private schools. These issues are a little easier for adoptive parents to control when their children are in elementary school settings. However, as the youngsters step into middle and high school, the parent becomes less directly involved and the adolescents begin to take more responsibility for their social life and peer interactions.

In individual sessions with teens, if we ask — the key word here is *ask* — about prejudices they face as a transracial teenager, they will talk openly. But usually they will only talk about it if they are directly asked. Teens growing up in transracial families usually mirror the characteristics of their adoptive family rather than their cultural/racial birth background. While a product of two backgrounds, the child primarily accepts the language, rituals, customs, values, and beliefs of the adoptive family.

As Alyssa commented in one session, "It's hard to feel connected to a history or people when I know very little about my ethnic background. I might look Korean, but I see myself as American. People, especially my teachers and kids at school that don't know me, base who I am on my appearance. They think if I look Asian, then I am Asian. They are totally wrong. I get mad that I am always having to explain myself. Also, you know about those stereotypes. Just because I am Asian does not mean I am good at math. I suck at math!"

It is important to help parents and their teens become strong advocates, particularly in the school environment. This can be challenging when the family has chosen to be less open about the adoption at school. Our experience is that the more openness and education about adoption within the school environment, the higher the probability that if these issues do surface at school they will be handled with accuracy and acceptance and assistance — just what the adolescent needs.

Differences become accentuated during adolescence. Parents must come to terms with the reality that their teenager's abilities and aspirations may not match their expectations. It is particularly important for adoptive parents to embrace their children's differences and create a sense of belonging for them in the family. Family therapy can help infertile parents grieve losses related to their fantasized biological children and promote their adopted children's self-esteem. Therapy can also help support parents who are parenting transracially or transculturally by giving practical advice about ways to meet their children's needs for connections with their race and culture. The therapist can also offer ideas about how to function as a multiracial or multiethnic family.

Beneath the Mask

Permanence

Like all children, adopted children need and want to know that they are loved and that the love is forever. However, adoptive parents may need to be encouraged to reinforce the issue of permanency more often. It may seem a little confusing to parents to do this when they are striving to help their teen leave the nest. Reassure them that it only appears to be a paradox. It is always easier to launch a daring adventure from a secure base.

Parenting adopted teens who are moving toward emancipation, leaving home for college, work, or other opportunities, presents some unique challenges. Often in late adolescence, the teen begins to ponder the longevity of the parent-child relationship and to think that because the adults have almost completed their job of raising them to young adulthood the relationship will soon come to an end. It is the responsibility of the parents to prepare the launching pad without creating fears of abandonment. We ran a support group that helped parents to more fully understand the underpinnings of separation and how the adopted teen may be especially vulnerable to separations of any kind. Listen to a few of the parents' observations.

Sam's mother was getting exasperated. She didn't understand her son. "I can't believe that I still have to tell Sam that I will be home at a certain time. He is almost eighteen years old and he seems to think one day I am just going to leave and never come home. I read about adopted kids worrying about losing yet another parent, but come on now, he should know after eighteen years I am not going anywhere."

Lynn's mom was also incredulous. "We were sitting one Sunday morning reading the paper and talking about how much fun it would be to have a place in the mountains. Lynn, age fifteen, came down the stairs and apparently had been listening to our conversation. As she approached us she had tears streaming down her face. She said, 'I knew you would leave me one day.'

"Leave her? Come on! We were just fantasizing about our dream retirement home! Where in the world would she come up with the idea that we would leave her?"

Another parent volunteered, "Three weeks before college applications were due, I walked into my daughter's room and she was sitting on her floor with papers strewn all over. She looked up at me and said, 'I can't do this.' I said, 'Do what?' She said, 'Go away. I don't want to leave you.' And then she started to cry. I did not know what to do. I felt so helpless. I was so surprised by my daughter. Everything was going along so smoothly."

Another father spoke up. "Our daughter has expressed negative feelings about her birth mother from time to time but mainly in the context of, 'How could she do that to me — abandon me like that?' A few months ago, she couldn't locate us. She tried calling all of our various phone numbers and she left messages. When we picked up one of her messages, we called her. She scolded us for not being available. She said, 'You know I have issues with abandonment.'"

Educating parents of teens about these dynamics can often prevent late adolescents from making some poor decisions that could have a negative impact on their future. Adoptive parents who are sensitive to these issues surfacing can open dialogue with their adolescent to affirm that they will always be their parents — no matter what.

The wonderful children's book written by Robert Munsch begins with a mother holding her new baby singing these words:

> *I'll love you forever*
> *I'll like you for always*
> *As long as I'm living*
> *My baby you'll be.*

Munsch depicts beautifully the permanency of a mother's love for her child. At the end of the story the mother is very sick and frail, and the son goes to his mother, picks her up, and sings:

Beneath the Mask

I'll love you forever
I'll like you for always
As long as I'm living
My mommy you'll be.

The fears around separation are not limited to the adolescent. They can also be felt by the parents. In fact, quite often in the treatment of adopted teens, parents enter therapy emotionally traumatized by the mere thought that their adolescent may actually search for birth parents. They fear that the information being requested and the thoughts and emotions stirred by the process of searching will threaten the stability of the family. It is imperative that the parents have an opportunity to express their fears and openly acknowledge them with their teen. The adolescents are typically cognizant of their parent's angst and need a forum in which to let them know that wanting more information and the possibility of searching does not mean that they do not and will not love their parents forever. They are surprised to learn that parents worry about this. After all, they believe they are the one anxious about abandonment, not their parents.

Adoptive parents need to be educated that the desire to begin the emotional search is a normal process for the adoptee and should be supported rather than thwarted. The therapist must help the parents accept that this is the teen's internal search for identity. As a rule, the fact that they are talking and thinking more about their birth parents does not mean that they want to go and find them. This is a process that may span years. In any case, even if the adolescent eventually decides they wish to conduct an actual search (which occurs in a minority of instances), this does not mean that the youngster wants to leave the adoptive parents. In fact, the turmoil that produces the urge to search requires increased support and guidance from the parents.

Some adopted teens and their parents have concerns about the future of family relationships as they anticipate the end of the active parenting stage. Teens may equate the normal task of separation with abandonment, and parents may be overly sensitive to rejection by their teens as part of the normal separation process. Family therapy can help parents and teens understand these complexities and navigate this stage more successfully.

Identity

Throughout this book we have spoken repeatedly about the adolescent's search for identity and the complexities adoption brings to the task of solidifying the self. We also must consider the identity of the adoptive parents and how their sense of self as parents can be shaken from time to time. Think about how often people outside of the adoption community make comments like these: "They are not Ben's real parents." "She must look like her real parents." "Who are the real parents?" These comments often resonate in the minds of adoptive parents, causing them to sometimes doubt that they are their youngster's real parents.

Adoptive parents are faced with identity issues throughout their journey of adoptive parenting and their status as parents is often challenged. Society is ambivalent about their "realness." Beyond society's ambivalence is the ambivalence that lies within the family itself. If you polled a cross section of adoptive parents they would tell you that somewhere along the way their parental identity has been challenged by their son or daughter. "You're not my real parents. I do not have to listen to you." "My real parents would let me sleep over my friend's house on a school night." "I hate your rules. I am going to live with my real parents." What an opening for the frequently rebellious adolescent!

● ●

CASE EXAMPLE

Mr. and Mrs. L sought therapy at our center because of concern about their daughter's depression and recent involvement in self-harming behaviors. Samantha, age

Beneath the Mask

fifteen, placed at age six, acknowledged her increasingly labile mood and feelings of hopelessness. During the initial assessment, she spoke of her overwhelming sense of sadness surrounding her adoption story. She described the death of her birth parents as a horrific loss. She was having great trouble coping with the reality that she would never see them again.

Several weeks later, Mrs. L came into the session furious with her daughter. Samantha had lied about a social activity and when her mother confronted her, Samantha got in her face and yelled, "You are not my real mother and will never be." Mrs. L started to cry and said ever since Samantha had been placed she would make this comment when confronted about misbehavior. Mrs. L described the tremendous pain and sadness these statements evoked. She acknowledged that her authenticity as a parent was stripped away each time Samantha lashed out at her in this way. She spoke of the inner turmoil it created for her and how she began to question her right to claim Samantha as her daughter. "What are we to her?" she asked. "Sometimes I feel so confused and conflicted."

Therapy enabled Samantha and her family to understand the depth of her unresolved grief and the purpose of the distancing behaviors that permeated her relationship with her parents. Grief work became the focus of Samantha's therapy. The therapist met individually with Mr. and Mrs. L to help them understand how grief is manifested in children and teens and to broaden their understanding as to why the comments surfaced around their role as parents. The therapist affirmed Mr. and Mrs. L's parental status and educated them about how not to get caught up in the frequently used adolescent manipulation of shouting "You're not my real parents" when issues of discipline surface.

During times of confrontation, parents must stay on track with setting limits. They must follow through and provide their teen with the message that right now they are talking about a rule that was violated, and that tomorrow, or even later that day, when they have settled the issue, feelings about adoption can be discussed. Parents need to take on this attitude, needed when parenting any adolescent, adopted or not: You can't blame a kid for trying, but the rules are the rules. All children, especially teenagers, need someone to set appropriate limits and boundaries. Children become scared when parents abdicate their responsibilities. The adolescent's true opinion, never voiced to the parent is this: If you loved me, you would take care of me and make sure I don't do things that will be harmful.

• •

In the case of the L family, therapy bolstered the parent's sense of entitlement and helped them to recapture the confidence that they were Samantha's parents. They came to understand that she needed them more than ever as she embarked on this painful journey of grief work.

Adoptive parents sometimes need assistance with their own identity and sense of entitlement as parents. Structural family therapy interventions are especially appropriate to empower parents who have issues with entitlement. Parents may also need help in understanding the identity issues facing their child, especially when the parents see the adolescent's interest in birth parents or other elements of history as a threat to their relationship with their child.

beneath the mask

Loyalty

Thoughts about birth parents may cause teens to feel disloyal to their adoptive family and conversely, love for one's adoptive parents can cause the youngster to feel disloyal to birth parents. Therapists working with adoptive families need to understand the delicate balance that the adolescent is trying to create between love for their adoptive parents and their increasing preoccupation with thoughts of their birth parents.

The parents may need help coming to terms with the notion that an adopted child's need to emotionally consider the significance of the other set of parents is by no means a reflection of diminishing feelings for the adoptive parents. It is this potential splitting of loyalties that often intensifies the anxieties within the adoptive parents as they fear their child will choose the birth parents over them. It is the level of these anxieties that often prevents the teen from openly discussing his emerging thoughts about his birth parents and the possible desire to eventually search for them. *Eventually* should be underscored here, as more often than not the teen has no intention of actually finding his birth parents. Rather, the adolescent is beginning to fantasize about what might happen if one day this should occur.

Adoptive parents need support to present clear and unconflicted messages to their teen, supporting the quest for information and possible future connections while voicing their honest feelings. Our clinical experiences at C.A.S.E. have shown us that teens are acutely aware of their parents' angst and they fret silently, fearing their parents will misunderstand their loyalties. An effective strategy for parents is to initiate conversation about birth parents and affirm their importance. This will show their teen that they are not afraid to talk about the birth parents. This removes the loyalty issues, or at least minimizes them.

For children placed at a later age, the issue of divided loyalties can be accentuated. These adoptive parents must be helped to understand that it is their responsibility to assist the adolescent in integrating the past and the present. Later-placed teens will have strong vivid memories of their birth families and therefore struggle on a more pervasive level with divided loyalties. Such adolescents often still desire to have connections to the individuals who were significant to them early in life. Adoptive parents are often astonished by the depth of the teens' continued emotional connection, and they are conflicted about supporting such attachments, especially if those individuals were abusive. Often they are very angry with these other adults who have mistreated the youngster they love.

● ●

CASE EXAMPLE

Irina was placed from an orphanage in eastern Europe at age twelve. During a family session, Irina spoke of her birth mother and her fond memories of her. Although Irina's mother knew that the reality of her past family life was being filtered through a self-created protective lens, she accepted her daughter's depiction of her birth mother and was able to let Irina see that she was comfortable with her talking about her mother. It was difficult, but Irina's mother consistently supported her daughter's need to embrace her birth mom.

This early acceptance of Irina's connection to her birth mom paved the way for Irina to work through all the unpleasant memories later in therapy when she felt safe enough to discard the rose-colored glasses she wore early in treatment. The therapist validated the adoptive mom's efforts and provided her with individual time to sort out her feelings. The therapist continued to educate Irina's mother as to the importance of showing acceptance of her daughter's feelings and helping her to clarify her emotions. Mom's acceptance gave Irina the message that she will never be judged negatively by her parents when she chooses to discuss her birth family.

In addition, an interesting dynamic in this case will further elucidate the variety of loyalty issues which may present themselves clinically when working with adoptive families. Irina had been placed along with her younger sister, Luba. Shortly after placement the parents learned from the girls that they also had an older sister living in Russia with a husband and young child. The girls were very attached to this sister who had visited them as often as she could while they were in the orphanage. However, the girls never had the opportunity to say good-bye to their sister.

Irina and Luba's parents were horrified to learn that the girls were now severed from this beloved family member. They quickly began the process of locating their sister Olga. Their search proved to be successful and ongoing communication is facilitated at this point through letter writing. It has been an amazing process to watch unfold as the girls' loyalty to such an important person in their lives is honored and protected. The family engages in individual and joint correspondence, and it's an exciting day when they find a letter from their older sister in the mailbox after school. The girls have shared their letters in therapy, proudly showing pictures of their extended family. They hope to be able to visit her some day. The parents have, in fact, tentatively scheduled such a trip in a year or two.

● ●

Relationship stresses can occur when adoptive parents fear the birth parents or when there is contact between the adoptive family and the birth family. When parental anxiety is conveyed directly or indirectly, it can create intense loyalty conflicts for the child, who already may struggle because of fantasies about or actual relationships with birth parents. Family therapy is an intervention that can provide the environment in which to safely explore these conflicts.

Remember our survey? We also asked parents what issues turned out to be significant in their teen's life. As noted previously, parents often do not identify adoption issues as the presenting problem. Clinicians are often required to listen to what is not being discussed regarding adoption in order to become more tuned into the fact that the presenting problems described by the parents may be obscuring the adoption related issues.

Each adoptive family treated will have incorporated the adoption experience in their own unique way and its meaning will be a collage of the perceptions of all members of the family. The therapist will need to join the family, viewing the adoption through their own personal kaleidoscope. Once the parents are engaged in therapy with their teen, they begin to see with some clarity the adoption issues that proved to be highly significant. The following list reflects the prominence of issues identified by parents in the survey:

- Early abandonment — 22
- Wanting more information about their adoption story — 15
- Wanting more information about their birth parents — 13
- Identity/search issues — figuring out who they are — 19
- Racial/cultural issues — 4
- Feeling different from peers — 6
- Questions that they received from others about their adoption — 1

Although the poll of parents is small, we believe the responses reflect the general population of adoptive families we treat in regard to the key adoption issues teens bring to the therapeutic experience. While extensive writings exist about other members of the adoption triad (that is, the adoptees and the birth parents) little data has been collected as to the adoptive parent's experience as they journey through the path of adoption. Adoption is a family experience and must be treated in this framework. It is vital to understand the developmental stages that adoptive parents move

Beneath the Mask

through along this journey, and we must begin to accept their inclusion in the therapeutic process when working with adopted adolescents. Conjoint and collateral sessions are highly indicated to help the teen along their journey.

I wondered how this box would ever help me, but I began making my family and relatives from clay, putting my hidden cries and fear inside. After I made all the family members I had lost, I closed my box as if I were saying good-bye for the very last time.
Irina

strategies That work

Group Therapy and other Therapeutic Techniques

Although therapists may have many techniques that they already use when working with adolescents, we have chosen several that we designed specifically to aid in the treatment of adoption issues. We hope these tools will be helpful to your clients as they have been to those at C.A.S.E.

GROUP THERAPY

Why groups? Groups offer a distinct advantage for adopted teens. By providing a social milieu for growth and emotional healing, adoptees can identify with other teens who are adopted and share similar feelings and thoughts about their adoption experience. This therapeutic setting can also be an invaluable place to release the stigma and secrecy that may still surround adoption in the teen's life. We often meet adoptees who have never had the opportunity to interface with other adoptees their age or who are living in family situations where it is not safe to share these powerful feelings.

Clinical experience reflects that the key therapeutic benefit of group work is the interaction among group members. (Lieberman, Yalom, and Miles, 1973). Interpersonal exchanges and feedback allow the participants to restructure their self-image and individual perceptions, ultimately validating the universality of their issues. For many of the adopted adolescents we have treated at C.A.S.E., the primary support of the group provided first of all a decrease in isolation. One adopted teenager said, "I always felt I was the only one who ever thought about what it would have been like to have been raised by my birth parents. What a relief it was to learn that such thoughts are common in adopted kids."

The groups also reinforce the universality of adoption. Another girl responded to group education by saying, "Wow, I am not the only person in the world who is adopted, in fact there are over five million people in the country who are adopted!" In these and other ways, the groups decrease the sense of being different from other youngsters. One Korean girl said, "I'm not the only one whose parents are a different race than myself."

● ●

CASE EXAMPLE

Kayley, whom we discussed in chapter 4, was referred to our center by her parents following individual therapy with a clinician who did not specialize in adoption. The parents were concerned that there had not been much progress in her treatment, which had followed a psychiatric hospitalization for suicidal ideation. At C.A.S.E. an initial assessment suggested that an integration of individual and group therapy would be the indicated treatment protocol, so Kayley was included in an adolescent girls group for adopted teens.

Beneath the Mask

Looking back on her experience, Kayley said that the group helped by affording her the opportunity to learn about others' adoption stories. "I found out that I was not alone and that there were similarities in all of our stories. I would have never gotten to hear other adopted kids' stories if I stayed with my old therapist. She just did not understand what I was going through.

"Many of us struggled with not having all the information about why we were placed for adoption and shared how incredibly upset we felt to not have a say in the decision of our adoption. We had no choice. I did not realize the depth of my anger until I came to this group. I was carrying around these thoughts, and the group helped me to identify the source of my rage. I was so angry all the time. I did not know why. The group helped me to figure this out.

"I learned that it was not my fault that I was placed for adoption and that I shouldn't be angry with myself. I had felt like I was not good enough — that my birth parents wanted a different kid, not me, and that's why I was adopted. I hated myself and found it hard to want to be alive. The group helped me to see that under all my anger was hurt — and the hurt was basically about why I was placed for adoption.

"This question wasn't answered for me but talking about it with other kids who really could understand my feelings was a big help. The group gave me support and allowed me to see I was not alone. I met other girls with problems too. Sometimes the group gave me the opportunity to see others' problems and compare them with my own. We shared our beliefs that our birth parents were not ready to take care of us. We decided together that they may have loved us and it was their love that gave them the courage to put us up for adoption."

● ●

Group Design

Parents who are seeking an adoption group for their child often want us to develop specialized groupings according to the type of adoption (that is, kids from foster care system, kids from a particular country, kids placed as infants, and so forth). Although we have conducted some homogeneous adoption groups, our experience has proven that the richness of a heterogeneous group is clinically preferable. What seems more important than the type of adoption in the design of the group is that the participants are close in development and share some common issues.

We have found that by including teens from all adoptive experiences — international, domestic, public child welfare, and others — we provide the group participants the opportunity to see the breadth of adoption. This allows the youngsters to normalize on a broad scale the similarities of issues. As one teen told another, "Wow, I know I had feelings about my birth mother because I lived with her for a short time, but I didn't think you would think about your birth mom since you came from Ethiopia. I guess we all think about our birth parents no matter where you were born."

The heterogeneous group also has a very practical advantage. From a logistical standpoint, unless you are treating large numbers of adoptees, it will be hard to arrange a homogeneous group — especially one that also considers developmental similarities and starts within a reasonable period after referral.

It is, of course, important to consider other expectations of the parents when evaluating teens for a group. As we've discussed, by this time in their development, the adolescent is processing the adoption experience in complex ways. Our group experience with teenagers creates interesting dynamics for parents. There tends to be heightened parental anxiety during the initial group assessment. Parents usually ask direct questions about the focus of the group and what will be discussed. One might think this is preposterous given the fact that the group is labeled an "adoption group." It seems fairly self-explanatory that adoption issues would be addressed. Remember, however, that parents of adopted teens begin to fear their teen will want to search for her or his birth parents and then choose them over their adoptive family. Some parents are also concerned that if their child talks about adoption the result will be disastrous for their child, themselves, or everyone.

Therapists may need to provide some extra education and dialogue to help alleviate parents' fears when trying to encourage them to accept the recommendation for a group experience. It will be important to spell out what issues typically arise in these types of groups. Parents need to know that experience has shown that virtually all of the youngsters will discuss their birth parents and often will come home and request more information from their parents. To that extent their expectations are accurate — those issues will be central in the group experience. However, the parents also need to be told that the reality is that the kids have been thinking about all these issues for some time. The group merely offers a safe, accepting place to utter the words. You can also reassure the parents that the open discussion of these thoughts, especially at home, is liberating for the entire family and healing for their child. These talks will not disrupt the family; they will solidify it.

Sometimes, when it becomes evident that the parents need a more structured format to explore their issues, we offer concurrent parent groups. If therapists decide this is necessary they will need an additional therapist to lead the parents' group. Therapists will also want to inform the adolescents that what they share in their group is confidential, and the same holds true for the parents. All participants need to know that there will be opportunity for sharing at the end of the group experiences.

Adolescents are frequently referred to groups at our center by psychotherapists who are providing individual therapy to the youngster. This can be a very productive experience for the patient if the two treating entities can work collaboratively. In your community there may be organizations such as C.A.S.E. that specialize in adoption-centered therapy and have developed a network within the adoption community. The opportunity for teens to have a group experience with other adoptees may be greater in a specialized center than in a private practice, where the caseload may not allow for an adoption group.

We have found that the individual therapist can continue working with the teen while we focus on the adoption issues. It is important for all the clinicians to have releases to collaborate so optimum benefit from both modalities can be achieved. We have also enjoyed this collaboration because it allows us to share our adoption knowledge with other mental health providers who may not have had the opportunity to focus on adoption in their practices. At the same time, the individual psychotherapist has a wealth of information that can enrich our understanding of the adolescent.

Pregroup Assessment

All teens being considered for the group attend a pregroup assessment interview with at least one parent. We conduct group assessments even if the adolescent is currently in individual or family therapy within our center. The interview is typically ninety minutes in duration and consists of a joint interview with the parents and teen and a period with the teen alone. The therapist explains the purpose of the group and reviews the group outline and projects the participants will engage in. In our groups, we use art, sand, and music therapy. We find that using a variety of clinical tools affords the optimum benefit from the group experience by having a variety of sensory, motor, and verbal modalities for kids who may have learning, attention, and processing challenges.

We are strongly convinced of the value — even the necessity — of preparing participants for groups. Pregroup interviews offer participants a systematic way to obtain information needed to enter a group experience. Given the adolescent's need for autonomy and sense of control this is particularly critical. Adolescents must feel

Beneath the Mask

that they have a say in the decision to enter the group. It is vitally important that each young person begins with some level of buy-in to the group launch. The worst case scenario for any clinician is to come face-to-face with a bunch of highly resistant teenagers who are skilled at sabotaging the group experience.

The second half of the pregroup assessment is with the teen alone. This allows an opportunity to explore both the youngster's feelings about the group as well as feelings and thoughts about the adoption experience. This is especially important if the youngster has not been seen before and is coming only for the group treatment. This chance to talk without the parents in the room can be very important since teens are often reluctant to share some of their internal and secret thoughts about adoption with the parents present.

During this private contact, the therapist can engage in some education with the teen, sharing general information about common thoughts and concerns other youngsters around the same age typically report about the adoption experience. This sharing can often engage a somewhat resistant teen who finds some comfort in the fact that there is a person who may truly understand what they have gone through as an adopted person. Finally, therapists should ask adolescents what they would like to get from participating in the group and encourage them to set a goal for themselves. As with any type of adolescent work, the therapist may be faced with a disengaged teen who presents with much resistance. The teen may have previously had a negative clinical experience or the mere thought of being thrust into such a close situation around personal issues with peers may be quite threatening. Our recommendation is to try to negotiate with the teen to commit to a few sessions with the option to stop if the experience is too overwhelming. While this may seem potentially disruptive to the cohesion of the group, in our experiences the adolescent rarely leaves the group.

The parent is then brought back into the interview, and the therapist affirms the teen's willingness to join the group and reviews the expectations of the group one more time. We are very careful to fully explain the purpose of the group and the expectations of the group before we ask for the definite commitment of both the teen and his or her parents. We work hard to minimize the possibility of group members dropping out of the group due to the sensitivity to loss issues and issues related to the birth parents. We believe we are most likely to avoid that outcome by adequately preparing the entire family for the intensity of emotion that is likely to be aroused in the group experience.

THE SCRIPTED GROUP SCHEDULE

At C.A.S.E. we have developed time-limited groups with a set curriculum for most of our clients. We also allow for flexible extended groups for those youngsters and families who need more extended treatment. It is important to note that while the following curriculum outline is designed for an eleven-week group, our experience with adolescents is that the groups tend to run over a twelve- to sixteen-week process. The groups are typically an hour and a half to two hours in duration, depending on the maturity of the teens. The issues outlined in the chart that follows are interwoven throughout the duration of the group. This approach can, of course, be tailored to the specific pattern of your own practice. We discuss some of the specific therapeutic techniques in greater detail later in this chapter.

THERAPEUTIC TOOLS FOR
INDIVIDUAL AND GROUP THERAPY

Like many others who have chosen to treat adolescents, we have learned that we must come prepared with a host of tools to enrich the therapeutic process and promote the greatest opportunity for self-exploration, insight, and engagement. In this section we explore a variety of therapeutic tools that we have found highly effective in exploring the complex issues inherent in adoption.

Table 6-1: Scripted Group Schedule

WEEK	TOPIC	CONTENT
One	Getting to Know One Another	Exploration of similarities and differences among our families and ourselves
Two	My Adoption Story	Through a creative art project, teens will create their adoption story to share with the group. The purpose of this exercise is to help the teen ascertain what information they do have and identify aspects of their story that need further elaboration and/or clarification. Sharing one's story is also a powerful normalizing process and helps the teen see that they are not alone.
Three	Emotions and Feelings	"Sometimes, I feel happy, sad, and angry all at the same time. It's confusing." Teens are encouraged to share the varying feelings they hold within themselves and to learn healthy ways to communicate these feelings.
Four	Birth Parents	"I think about my birth parents, but am afraid to tell anyone. I have lots of questions I would like to ask them." Teens are encouraged as a group to create a "puzzle" of questions they would like to have answered by their birth parents.
Five	Birth Parents, Part 2	Teens grapple with the relinquishment decision during adolescence. In order to gain a deeper understanding as to the complexities of the relinquishment decision, teens read together *The Mulberry Bird*, by Anne Brodzinsky (1996).

continued on p. 150...

...continued from p. 149

Table 6-1: Scripted Group Schedule (continued)

WEEK	TOPIC	CONTENT
Six	Identity	"Who am I? Who am I like? Who do I identify with?" Through the use of The Game of Discovery, an interactive exercise created especially for adoptees. This game assists teens to understand that their identity is based upon characteristics from their birth parents, adoptive parents and self. "What makes me unique — how am I different from and like my parents — birth and adopted?" How do I put this all together?
Seven	Identity, Part 2	Mask Making: what do we show on the outside and what we keep in the inside.
Eight	Relationships	Fears of intimacy related to abandonment and rejection often affect the teen's ability to establish and maintain healthy peer relationships. Issues of sexuality surface as they further try to understand the nature of their birth parent's relationship: "Did my birth mother mean anything to my birth father?" "Did they love one another?" "Should I have sex before marriage?" "If you are going to be sexual, then you better take responsibility!"
Nine	Relationships, Part 2	Making healthy choices for myself. "Trust" — what it is and how to get it! "Will everyone leave me?"

continued on p. 151...

Sharing Keepsakes

In joining the teens along their journey of self-awareness, we often ask them to bring in any photo albums, pictures, and memorabilia that

Beneath the Mask

...continued from p. 150

Table 6-1: Scripted Group Schedule (continued)		
WEEK	TOPIC	CONTENT
Ten	W.I.S.E. UP!^{SM}	"Why do people ask me so many questions about my adoption?" Participants are taught the W.I.S.E. UP!^{SM} program (discussed in detail later in this chapter) to empower them with choices as to how they want to respond.
Eleven	Family Night (optional, depending on the group)	This is an opportunity for teens to share with their parents highlights of adoption issues that were important to them over the course of the group and also, an opportunity in a safe, structured environment for teens to acknowledge the importance of these issues in their life.

represent different aspects of their adoption story. This is an invaluable tool as you assist the teens in their understanding of their adoption experience. It's a great group technique because it provides teens with a launching point for telling their stories. Be prepared to accept all kinds of things kids may bring in. You might be surprised at the items teens hold close to their hearts as they put the pieces of their puzzle together.

CASE EXAMPLE

Justin, age thirteen, was experiencing a great deal of conflict about his relinquishment and was very angry that his birth mother had abandoned him. He had begun to distance himself socially, and his performance at school was deteriorating. Justin could not understand why *any* mother would just walk away from her baby and leave him forever. Now that he was thirteen, he felt that his birth mother could have figured out a way to keep him. He felt strongly that being young was no excuse. He was adamant about this. Justin was participating in a teen group, and on one particular evening the kids were asked to bring in anything they wanted to share about their adoption. This is a common task that usually occurs in the first few weeks of the group. The following week Justin brought in a small box, which he cradled carefully. After several teens shared their treasures, Justin slowly opened his box. Resting on an old piece of cotton was a shriveled-up, small, brown item. Justin went on to explain that this was a piece of his umbilical cord, the only thing that he had to connect himself to his birth mother — both literally and figuratively. Justin stared at the dried-up tissue and began to sob. "Why did she have to leave me?" he moaned.

● ●

Birth Parent Puzzle Mural

Irina wrote, "Being adopted is like being a puzzle — except there is a missing piece!" Becca commented, " I am thankful I was adopted but … it's so hard to live with the missing piece of the puzzle, it's never complete!" The puzzle as a metaphor for describing how adoption feels to adoptees is reflected in adoption literature and in our countless interviews and therapeutic sessions with adopted children and teens.

The purpose of this activity is to help teens identify questions about their birth families in order to normalize thinking and fantasizing about them. First you should introduce the idea of birth parents. It is highly probable that discussions of birth parents have already surfaced in the contextual framework of the group. If not, you may want to stimulate the discussion by introducing questions and thoughts other teens you have worked with have had about their birth parents and how normal and common this is.

Give each teen at least four large cut-out puzzle pieces and instruct them to write questions they would like to have answered about their birth parents. After individual members have completed their pieces, instruct them to attach a piece to another group member's piece to eventually form an entire puzzle. There is no set order regarding the connection of pieces.

You can then ask them to glue all the pieces onto a large piece of butcher paper. If they choose to, they can develop a title for the group puzzle. Then you should proceed with an overall group discussion about the questions they posed and how others may have similar questions or completely different ones. Some of the questions may have never entered some of the participants' minds before this exercise. Thus this exercise may elicit new feelings and thoughts. It is important to acknowledge with the teens that some questions may never be answered and some can be answered through information that the adoptive parents hold but have not shared. Other questions must wait until the adolescent can legally search. Still, there will always be gaps; it is unavoidable. It is always important to explore feelings around the unknown. This exercise usually requires two group sessions. It can also be used for a final session with the teens and parents, either as an individual family group or as an exercise for a final multifamily group session.

The following questions were developed by a group of eighth graders who attended our eight-week Kids Adoption Network Group℠. These are the questions on their puzzle:

- What instrument do you play?
- How tall are you?
- What are you doing now?
- What do you know about me?

- How would you feel if I told you to get lost?
- Where do you live?
- What did you work at?
- How would you feel if I came back to Russia to see you?
- Does my birth mom think about me?
- Are my birth parents like me?
- Did my birth father pick me up?
- What did my birth father look like?
- I want to know if you loved me.
- Do you have other kids?
- Why did you born me?
- What was my birth dad's name?
- What does my birth mother look like now?
- Does my dad look like me? And my mom?
- When did they have me?
- Do they remember me?
- How old is my brother?

We have found the use of a puzzle to be a significant therapeutic tool in helping adoptees to acknowledge the missing pieces of their story and to identify the questions that occupy their minds surrounding their adoption.

● ●

CASE EXAMPLE

Rachael, a fourteen-year-old adolescent, had been in therapy since age seven; her parents referred her to help support their daughter, who has a very difficult adoption story. Rachael was abandoned in a trash bag in a Dumpster shortly after her birth. She was found by a local storekeeper, who was putting out his trash. Because of the nature of this situation, the community was made aware of the abandoned child in the hope of locating the birth mother. Rachael's adoptive parents had been open and honest with her from the beginning and slowly shared aspects of her story when it was developmentally appropriate.

Rachael continues to access therapeutic support and re-enters therapy when issues arise. Over a year ago Rachael requested to return to therapy as she was struggling with some issues related to her adoption. She stated that she had been doing a lot of thinking and that she was very worried about something. She shared that she had a personal dream to one day become president of the United States and that this could never happen because when people looked into her past and found out about how she had come into this world they would not vote for her. Rachael was carrying a tremendous burden with far-reaching implications. As she articulated her feelings and concerns, it became clear that Rachael was pondering many questions about her adoption and felt very confused and shamed by the circumstances of her abandonment. Her concern about her candidacy for the presidency revealed her feeling that the entire nation knew of her horrible abandonment. She felt overwhelmed by the potentially far-reaching implications of her relinquishment and ashamed of her origins.

Since Rachael is an artistic teenager who enjoys self-expression through art, the puzzle seemed to be an appropriate clinical intervention at this stage in her treatment. (See figure 6.1 in appendix A for a picture of Rachael's puzzle.) She wrote the following questions on her puzzle pieces:
- Where are they right now?
- Why do I reap the consequences for their choices?
- Who am I really?
- Why do I still feel like it is my fault?
- What could I have done to change it?

- Why is my life is complicated for things I had no choice about?
- Why me?
- Why couldn't I stay with my biological parents?
- Why would they choose to abandon me?

Rachael felt that the puzzle was helpful to her as she gained more clarity by actually visualizing her thoughts and feelings through the experience of making the puzzle. "I felt relieved when I could talk about and write down the questions without having to come up with a solution. I learned that I did not always have to have an answer to every question. The puzzle also helped me to realize that all the pieces would eventually come together even if I did not have all the answers. Some puzzles take longer than others, and I realized that this puzzle wasn't like the ones I did as a little kid. It was much bigger than that and would probably take my whole life to put together. I then became willing to work on the puzzle to benefit myself in a way that would help to make me a better and stronger person as a whole.

"The puzzle was an easy way to make my feelings and thoughts visible so that one by one my questions could get answered. I soon was able to answer some and leave the others to be answered another time or not be answered at all. I became okay with that even though it was very hard. I spent a lot of time convincing myself that it was okay that all the questions weren't answered because I was still a whole person even if the puzzle was not whole.

"I remember that when the questions were answered we put a little dot on the puzzle by those that were answered. There were nine pieces to my puzzle with one question on each. I have a dot next to two of those pieces.

The questions on the pieces were 'Why do I feel like it is my fault?' and 'What could I have done to change it?' To answer the first, I found that what affects me isn't always my fault and I came to the realization that it was indeed not my fault at all because I was just an unborn infant at the time. I knew that no matter how I was I couldn't affect another person's thoughts without being there. To answer the second, I found that I couldn't have done anything to change it, so I just needed to stop thinking that I could have. I realized that I wasn't superwoman and never would want to be. I just wanted to be me, with all the things that came along with it, no matter how painful they may be."

● ●

By using the puzzle medium, Rachael could safely identify the questions surrounding her abandonment and begin to confront the complexities each one raised as she worked toward coming to terms with the painful aspects of her story. We believe it would have taken many months or longer for her to verbally articulate these issues without the use of this treatment tool. Many adopted teens assume a tremendous sense of responsibility for decisions that were made by others and suffer senseless shame as a result. Therapy must help them to absolve themselves of this burden; it is not theirs to carry.

Reading and Discussion

The array of adoption literature now available, particularly books geared to children and teens, can be an enriching resource to use therapeutically. Sharing adoption-related books with adolescents during therapy can help to normalize their feelings by exposing them to the experiences of other adoptees. Sometimes just reading the words written by other adopted persons validates the teens' feelings and can help to reduce their feelings of isolation and differentness. Furthermore, books can educate the teens, providing answers to questions that they may have surrounding the adoption process and the impact on other members of the adoption triad. In group therapy, books can lead to lively, stimulating discussions and at the same time serve an educational purpose. (appendix B includes a bibliography of titles we have found helpful.)

The Game of Discovery: Who Am I?

If the walls of our therapy rooms could speak, they would resonate with the sounds of teens asking, "So who am I? — really!" How do we as clinicians begin to help them sort through what they do know, what they do not know, what they wish they knew, and what they will never know in order to develop a sense of self? We must help them internalize two sets of parents in formulating their identities. As Nydam (1999, 48) so eloquently described this integration: "The adoptee's identity is the fruit from two trees."

To help teens along their search for self we created The Game of Discovery℠, which can be used individually or in group therapy. You will need a canvas bag filled with star-shaped characteristics of self, such as hair color, personality traits, food preferences, and so forth. The participants use a spinner and move around a circular board with spaces labeled "Adoptive Parents," "Birth Parents," "Myself." When a player lands on a labeled space, they pick a piece from the canvas bag and discuss where they believe the characteristic came from — their birth parents, adoptive parents, or themselves. Any other player can choose to challenge them and voice their opinion about the trait's origin. This game can be played with two or more players.

As we developed this book we asked our teens what clinicians needed to know about adoption so they can be more effective with their clients. Becca said emphatically, "They need to be able to support us in figuring out who we are. Ignorance is not bliss in adoption! How do you figure out who you are or who you can become

Beneath the Mask

when you don't have all the information? You can't get a picture of yourself. What did you inherit? What is learned? What has to do with your adoptive family?"

This simple game is a wonderful tool to help teens explore the origins of who they are and where certain characteristics came from. We have had countless lively, thought-provoking sessions using the Game of Discovery as adoptees ponder how they became who they are. There have been many touching opportunities to share thoughts with one another about where the different elements of each unique trait might have originated — from their birth parents, from their adoptive family and, finally, which personality parts may simply have originated in them.

We also find this tool to be helpful to use with parents. It allows parents to see the importance of the birth family in their child's identity formation and provides them the opportunity to explore how an adopter's sense of self is the integration of themselves as adoptive parents, birth parents, and the unique characteristics that the teen brings as well. We have introduced this tool in parent educational forums as well as in family therapy.

Mask Making

As our work with teens has evolved, the use of masks has grown as a significant therapeutic tool. The masks used for this book were created by clients in our center and represent their inner thoughts, feelings, and perceptions about who they are — how they see themselves and how they believe or want others to see them. Some teens are so confused about their identity that the mask making affords them the opportunity to begin to solidify those aspects of themselves that they feel uncertain about. The masks also can reveal "faces" that have been hidden or used as protective shields.

We have found that purchasing precut and formed masks is ideal. The teens are given a wide range of art materials — paints, pastel chalks, charcoal, feathers, jewels, glitter, and so forth — to create their masks. Many teens will engage in dialogue during the mask-making process; others prefer silence, which should be respected. Following the completion of the mask, processing is always encouraged.

W.I.S.E. UP!^{SM}

Over the years we have learned from adoptees of all ages that one of the most challenging and painful aspects of being adopted is how frequently they are asked intrusive, hurtful questions. Sometimes the questions or comments are related to the adopter's personal adoption story. In other cases, they are asked to be the in-house adoption expert — to comment on news, events, movies, and TV shows related to adoption. The children and teens we have worked with have shared how difficult and uncomfortable this makes them feel because they often do not know what to say. Afterward, they often regret what they did say. Frequently the questions are ones that they have not yet thought through, so the questions lead them to a place where they are not yet prepared to venture.

A person who is not adopted cannot begin to understand the power of these questions and the feelings they evoke. Walk in the shoes of the adopted child for a minute. Slowly read this list of questions that are frequently posed to our clients. Read the list aloud.

- Where is your real mother? How come she did not keep you?
- Don't you want to find your real mother?
- I heard you were left in an orphanage. What was wrong with you?
- Do you have a dad? Where is he? How come he didn't marry your mother?
- Is your mother a prostitute?
- What does it feel like to be adopted?
- Do you have brothers or sisters?
- I heard that all kids in foster care were abused. What happened to you?
- How do you know what you will look like when you grow up?

- How can that be your mother? Her skin isn't dark like yours.
- How much did your parents pay for you?
- Is your real mother a drug addict?
- What did your parents tell you about why they chose adoption? How did it make you feel?
- What does adoption mean to you?
- Do you know anyone else who is adopted?
- What is one thing you think other kids who are adopted have in common?
- How often do you think about adoption?
- Do you ever feel less loved by your relatives?

Well, what do you think? What did this feel like to you? Did you think about how you would answer such questions? Did you ponder why someone would ask these questions? Can you imagine a seven-, nine-, or fifteen-year-old answering these questions?

Adoptees hear these questions on the basketball court, in the locker room, at lunch, in the school hallways, in the classroom, at a sleepover party, and at family gatherings. They are posed by friends, acquaintances, strangers, teachers, friends' parents, and coaches. They come without advance warning. They may be delivered in innocence, derisively, demandingly — each form presents its own challenge.

To empower adoptees to deal with these questions, we use the W.I.S.E. Up program created by Marilyn Schoettle, M.A., at C.A.S.E. "These questions often go right to the heart of an adoptee's self-concept, challenging who they are and where they belong. The W.I.S.E. Up program not only empowers children to take control, it helps them to understand they are *wiser* than other people about adoption. The program empowers adopted kids to help others learn more truthful, positive information about adoption" (Schoettle, 2000).

The W.I.S.E. Up program teaches effective techniques for helping kids deal with the painful and often disturbing encounters with others who are undereducated about adoption. C.A.S.E. has published the *W.I.S.E. Up Powerbook* to provide children and teens with practical guidelines as to how to handle any question or comment about adoption. *The Powerbook* can be purchased with a parent and or clinical guide that provides details about how to use the program individually with clients and or in a group experience. The program is simple and easy for children and teens to remember. They are taught that they have four choices:

W Walk away or choose not to pay attention
I It's private: I can choose not to share information
S Share some information about adoption or my story
E Educate others about adoption in general, by telling them correct information and helping them understand it

The details of the program and collaborative guides are too lengthy to be included in this book, but the publications can be ordered through the C.A.S.E. Web site at http://www.adoptionsupport.org. Over the years we have trained hundreds of children to use the program, empowering them to take control and see that they have choices as to how they wish to respond to and share personal information about their adoption stories. After learning how to use this program teens have communicated how helpful the program has been to them when faced with challenging questions.

The Loss Box
The concept of the Loss Box was not created by C.A.S.E. It has been used in other treatment modalities, and we have found it to be a very helpful tool in working with grieving children. We use it to guide teens through the psychological task of grief work. Because loss is such a paramount entity in adoption, we evaluated many loss models. Eventually we chose the work of Dr. Maria Trozzi (1999) as our conceptual framework for grief and loss work with children. Trozzi

identifies four psychological tasks of grief work: understanding, grieving, commemorating, and moving on.

We are struck again and again by the number of adolescents we treat who are struggling with unresolved grief and loss issues surrounding their adoption. The losses are profound and, at times, psychologically debilitating. Many teens who come into therapy with a diagnosis of anxiety disorder, a mood disorder, or post-traumatic stress disorder are in fact suffering from what was once called a missed grief reaction. They have never had therapeutic support and guidance allowing them to mourn their losses so that they can move forward. This clinical picture is especially common in children from our public child welfare systems and children coming out of institutions all over the world. These are children who have losses that we adults could never imagine. Some of these teens will require the specialized techniques described in chapter 7, where we address the treatment of those with traumatic childhood experiences. For most of the adolescents we serve, the Loss Box has been a critical tool in helping them move through the stages of grief.

Initially, most teens find the weight and magnitude of their losses overwhelming. The teens cannot stop thinking about the people, places, and things ripped away from them. They are often plagued by constant worries that something terrible will happen again, to either themselves or their new family. The grieving teens often present clinically as highly anxious, inattentive, and behaviorally challenging. Their grief is taking over their lives and interfering with day-to-day experiences. The Loss Box literally serves as containment by giving boundaries to the losses. The Loss Box provides the opportunity to identify and acknowledge their losses. The adolescent uses this exercise to experience the painful feelings associated with the loss and then to gain some mastery over their emptiness and grief by symbolically re-creating what they lost. The exercise also provides a way to honor and commemorate the persons, places, or things they lost. Eventually, the Loss Box offers symbolic closure and a way for saying good-bye and moving on. This ceremonial farewell can be important since many of the teens we see never had the opportunity to say good-bye to lost loved ones.

To initiate the use of this tool, the therapist typically dialogues with the teen about the power of their losses upon their lives and the impact it is having by not getting in touch with those uncomfortable feelings connected to their losses. The therapist tells the teen that they have a very helpful project that they can participate in to begin to carefully and slowly explore the important things that they have lost. The teens are given the opportunity to pick out a simple shoe box (we have a large supply in our offices) and they are encouraged to decorate the box any way they would like. It is their box — their Loss Box. We provide an array of art materials: tissue paper, fabric, paint, glitter, markers, glue, jewels, string, yarn, stickers, and so forth. As the teen decorates the box, we talk about the purpose of creating this box.

When the decorating is completed, we carefully guide them in beginning to identify their losses. As they identify each loss, the teen is encouraged to share their "understanding" of why this loss occurred. Each acknowledged loss is then recreated through some artistic expression — drawing, collage, writing (poems, words, thoughts), clay work, and so forth. During the creation process the therapist helps the teen explore what was significant about this person, place, or thing and gives permission for the teen to talk about what it feels like to have lost what was so important. This provides teens with the opportunity to grieve their losses in a safe, nurturing, supportive environment and in a way that is developmentally appropriate.

Initially, the teen may only be able to tolerate identifying one loss. It is very important to allow the teen to proceed at an emotional pace that is safe for them. Some teens, particularly those placed at an older age, have experienced so much trauma and loss that the losses quickly pour out when they are given the opportunity to acknowledge them. If that is the case, allow them to do so, but slow down the process of exploration. You must be careful not to allow an overloading of grief to surface as it can be dangerous clinically. The teen often does not have the internalized coping skills to deal with such a powerful flooding of emotions. In some cases, you may observe a teen dissociate as the trauma is too powerful for them to hold in memory at that particular time. Slowing down the process will often allow them to use memory adaptively so that they can enter a space of comfort and safety. If dissociation does occur, it is helpful to ask the teen where they are to discover more about where they go mentally when the world seems too overwhelming. (We discuss dissociation further in chapter 7.)

Using the Loss Box is a slow process. It is not a tool to use in one session. It is a technique to utilize periodically throughout the therapy with teens suffering from unresolved losses.

Once the teen can identify and begin to experience the painful feelings associated with the losses, he or she can move on to what Trozzi (1999) calls "commemorating" the losses. This is the emotional state in which kids can remember the persons, places, or things that are not a part of their lives anymore. This stage affords the young person the ability to finalize and have partial closure to their past. It is here that the therapist will want to offer probing questions to aid in this process. Teens will often look to therapists for guidance as to what they can do to commemorate their losses. We have seen teens write poems about loved ones, create a memorial garden, write prayers, and develop rituals around the anniversary of the loss to remember those they loved.

In time the teen can and will move on. Trozzi (1999, 67) explains, "Going on involves a transformation over time in which children learn that the pain of grief subsides and the legacy of their loved one lies within themselves."

CASE EXAMPLE

First of all, my name is Irina. I was adopted three and a half years ago from Russia. My parents have provided for me so much and love me so much, all I can say is kind THANK YOU. In the past I have been struggling with serious loss in my family in Russia and I have also suffered depression. I did not know what to do. My mother asked some advice from adoptive moms and her friends about which therapist would be best for the first time. I had no idea what I am supposed to do — maybe sharing my feelings with her or just be silent? It took me a while to trust her with my personal story that happened in Russia. I came to a point where I could not hold my deep and hurtful feelings, so I HAD TO LET THEM GO!

Miss Deb and I talked about some helpful ways to let go of my pain. On the next few weeks Mrs. Deb and I came up with a lost box. It is just a box! I pondered deeply how in the world this box is going to help me?! I decided to decorate my lost box with bright color — fuchsia. This color represents my favorite dress that I wore a lot in Russia as a little girl. Finally, Mrs. Deb and I talked about how many people I have passed away. I began making my family and relatives from clay with hidden cry and fear inside, knowing that I will never see them again on this earth. After I made all of my family members, I closed my box as if I where saying good-bye for the very last time. Most challenging experience for me was that I never said good-bye to my family members, especially to my beloved mother. I said to myself one day that I have to let this go because it will not help me with my dilemma with grief. So I let it go — it was the most arduous decision that I ever made! The box has truly helped me to discover who I am. My advice for those who are struggling with loss in everyday life, you can make a box — take a shoe box and decorate it! I find this method very helpful and it helped me to understand that I am not alone in the world that is struggling with loss and grief. Make a good decision! Have fun making your box!

(Irina's loss box is pictured in figure 6.2 in appendix A.)

● ●

Writing and Journaling

For some teens, documenting their thoughts as they use therapy to assist them in resolving adoption issues may be of value. We keep blank journals at our offices and give these to any youngsters who use writing as a medium for self-expression. The teens often like to decorate their journals and may or may not chose to share their writings in therapy. Other forms of writing — particularly poetry — have been a prominent expressive tool for our young people.

complicated
BY Elyse, Age 13

I feel lost and lonely
But I don't know why
I feel hopeless and worthless
I can see it in my own eyes
There's this place in my mind
Where I wish I could hide
I can't believe how many times I have lied
To my friend and family
Even to myself
I feel confused and enraged

I'm trapped in this cage
Where no one can see me
What's happening to me?
There is one place at the end of this rope
It holds nothing but my fear and hope.
I can't understand why I am feeling this way
But I only wish that it would go away
I miss all those moments
When it use to be
It was nothing but my friends and me
Everything was right
But now it is all wrong
I feel like this emptiness is becoming too long
No one understands how much I have done
And what I am going through

Although this is not an exhaustive list of treatment tools, we hope it has provided some additional mediums for engaging teens in therapy. We find these tools can make the process of sorting through adolescents' varying emotions and thoughts about their adoption experience less threatening. The issues surrounding adoption are often complex and confusing for the teen. Therapists must step beyond the realm of a purely didactic exchange and utilize as many creative techniques to engage the adolescent and facilitate their understanding. These techniques can safely help to break down barriers and invite the adolescent to become an active partner along this therapeutic journey.

My therapist helped me to face my fears, find a solution to my problems, and relate it to my past. No one ever wanted to talk about my past before.

Jane

CHAPTER 7

No Expiration Date on Memories

working with

Traumatized Adolescents

As the face of adoption continues to evolve, individuals and couples are choosing to adopt older children, both domestically and internationally. Such children have often experienced years of abuse, neglect, and deprivation. Although adoption agencies try to educate prospective adoptive parents about the risks associated with children placed at an older age, the desire to become a parent often overrides the reality of problems that are likely when adopting an older child from either an orphanage or the public child welfare system.

Much has been written in the adoption literature about attachment and its implication for adoption adjustment. Put simply, attachment occurs when an affectionate bond develops as a result of continuous, positive, pleasurable, need-satisfying interactions between a child and consistent caretaker. Bowlby postulated that if children are not provided with the opportunities to form healthy, secure attachments early in life, emotional problems will persist, impeding the formation of intimate enduring relationships (Bowlby, 1969, 1978).

Attachment theorists stress the importance of early parent-child bonds as the foundation for healthy psychological adjustment spanning the development and growth of the individual. When this process is thwarted, the impact upon the individual can be devastating, affecting their ability to form healthy attachments. A growing number of adoption theorists have focused on the impact of severed attachments upon the adoption adjustment of children placed after the first year of life and those who have had multiple caregivers and experienced abuse, neglect, and trauma prior to being placed in a permanent family (Brodzinsky, Smith and Brodzinsky, 1998; Fahlberg, 1991; Keck and Kupecky, 1995).

Our experience reinforces to us that childhood abuse, neglect, and trauma inherently perpetuate disruptions in attachment. Because so much has already been written about attachment issues in adoption, we do not focus on that here; instead, we explore the complexities of treating adopted adolescents whose lives have been touched by multiple traumas. At such young ages our clients have experienced more trauma and loss than most adults we know. They have been ripped from their families, experienced serious neglect, abused sexually and physically, witnessed violence, and faced with the death of loved ones.

As a result of these circumstances, many of the children we treat have been misdiagnosed — or carry a variety of diagnoses — before the diagnosis of complex post-traumatic syndrome is identified. These are adolescents who may present with self -injurious behaviors, depression, anxiety, anger management issues, substance abuse, and relational problems. Because early life histories are often lacking, one cannot rely on a thorough social-developmental assessment. Formulating an effective treatment plan for this special population can be challenging, particularly when therapists have nothing to substantiate their suspicion of trauma.

Beneath the Mask

CASE EXAMPLE

Jane, a beautiful, bright, twelve-year-old, was placed in her adoptive family at age five after spending time in an orphanage in Eastern Europe. Jane was referred by her placement agency after her parents reported growing difficulties in parenting her. Jane's parents reported an increasing frustration with their daughter, who was becoming more defiant and withdrawn. The parents had two birth children close in age to Jane, and they were also being emotionally affected by Jane's recent oppositional behaviors and disregard for family rules and values. Her parents were confused as to why these behaviors/problems were appearing now, seven years after placement. Both Mom and Dad communicated their attachment and love for Jane, but they could not tolerate her violation of family rules and the disrespect she showed them.

Jane presented as a controlled, defended preteen who was guarded and lacked insight into her current behavioral presentation. Jane was clingy toward her mom and ambivalent toward her father's relationship with her. Individual and conjoint family therapy was initiated. The family therapy focused on helping everyone communicate their expectations and set realistic goals surrounding behavior management. The parents were provided with constructive coping strategies, and the therapist reinforced safety within the family, stressing no physical punishments. Providing the parents with a place to sound out their concerns reduced the stress level dramatically within the household.

During one family session, someone commented on the fact that Jane seemed tired all the time. The parents could not identify any sources for her tiredness and the parents stated that all the children went to bed at a reasonable time. They were baffled as to why Jane was so tired all the time. Jane's sleep habits were explored with her during an individual therapy session. It became clear to the therapist that while Jane did go to bed at the same time her siblings did, she was not sleeping at night.

It has been well documented that individuals who have experienced previous trauma are often functioning in the hyper-arousal response stage and report sleep disturbances similar to Jane's. These individuals report difficulty in actually falling asleep within a reasonable time period, describe themselves as being light sleepers, and reveal that they wake up more often throughout the night. Many patients describe that when they do fall asleep, their sleep is filled with nightmares (Herman, 1992).

Pulling from clinical presentations from other cases of later placed adolescents with similar sleep disturbances, the therapist began to explore past sleeping rituals within the orphanage. She asked Jane where she slept in the orphanage and asked her to draw a picture of her bed in the orphanage, as she suspected a correlation between the sleep problem and events at the orphanage. Jane drew a picture of many beds next to each other and pointed out which one was her own. Jane went on to explain that in the orphanage once you got into bed, you were not allowed to leave your bed, no matter what — you could not go to the bathroom, get up if you were sick or just scared. You were taught to remain in your bed. If you left your bed you were punished.

Jane spoke of being very scared at nights in her new home and shared that her parent's bedroom was far down the hall. There were nights where she needed them but was afraid to get out of bed, as she believed she would get punished as she experienced in the orphanage. Jane's parents had no idea that their daughter had been traumatized by situations within the orphanage and that these memories were keeping her from feeling safe and secure at home.

To alleviate her anxieties and show her that her parents wanted to respond to her at night and that she would not be punished, the therapist instructed Jane to cut up strips of colored paper during one session. At the following family session, the parents were given the strips and told for the next two weeks to come to Jane's bedroom every evening and leave two strips of colored paper on her floor beside her bed. The parents did this for two weeks and Jane would come into therapy beaming holding a handful of brightly colors strips. "See what I found on my floor," boasted Jane, "I am so happy. My parents came every night to check on me and never got angry with me."

In following sessions Jane was asked to call her parents several times from her room to see that they would come as well. She was also encouraged on a few occasions to get out of her bed and go to her parent's room to practice when in the future she may need them for something. At first Jane was very reluctant to leave her bed and spoke of fears associated with orphanage life. In time she overcome these fears and felt very secure that if she needed her parents they would come without any punishment.

Jane's behavioral problems dissipated as well as her sleeping issues. She became less anxious and rebellious. Her parents were very relieved to learn the underpinnings of their daughter's behaviors and showed much more sensitivity to her emotions now that they had a clearer understanding of her previous life experiences. Even though the initial symptomatology was treated, Jane continued therapy on a less frequent basis. She found the support of therapy helpful when her anxieties began to increase, which often occurred when she was faced with new situations and transitions. The full extent of her traumas are still unknown; however, she and her family accept the fact that staying connected to therapy is extremely important so as to support her when new memories surface or life events trigger previous trauma.

A year after Jane began therapy, the therapist was to speak at an annual conference for international adoption agencies. The therapist told her that she was presenting on issues related to children who were adopted when older and asked her if she would write something that would help to raise their awareness as to the challenges facing kids who had lived in orphanages. She came back the following week and handed the therapist this writing:

In the Russian orphanages we weren't allowed to get out of bed at night. So one day I started to have many sleeping troubles and I was too scared to get out of bed. Once I told my therapist she took complete action. We did some activities for me to understand that I was safe and how to stay calm and get up to tell my parents I was scared or couldn't sleep. I had finally one night become brave enough to get out of my bed and I told my parents that I couldn't sleep. Not only did my therapist help me to accomplish this action, she also helped me think of ways on how I might fall asleep and relax myself. She also supported my parents during a very frustrating time. Later on I did overcome my sleep problems. As an eleven year old I think that it can be important at certain times and depending on your situation to have such as place as C.A.S.E. This can be helpful because the counselors know what adoption is like after much experience

and handling so many cases. I myself had two types of coun-
selors, one for everybody and one just for adopted kids. We
talked about many things and either way they led up to
adoption questions, fears, happiness, and difficulties. My
therapist helped me to face my fears, find a solution to my
problems and relate it to my past. No one before wanted to
talk about my past.

Jane, now age fourteen, is currently experiencing great happiness and success in her life. She is excelling academically, has many friends, loves her family, and wants all to know that she has not been back to therapy for two years

● ●

THE THERAPEUTIC ALLIANCE

The past cannot be ignored when working with teens who have been placed at an older age, typically ages seven and older. Too often, parents, professionals, and some therapists believe that children can and should forget the past. In fact it would be easier for all involved if we could just close that chapter in their lives and help them to begin to build new ones. People always say that children are resilient. But I sit with the pain and suffering of these young people day in and day out and I often ask myself, what is that suppose to mean? According to the Merriam-Webster dictionary (2001), *resilience* means "the ability of a strained body to recover its size and shape after deformation caused especially by compressive stress; the ability to recover from or adjust easily to misfortune or change."

The ability of the body to recover is not a simple task for anyone whose life has been darkened by trauma. This is particularly true for children. It is our experience that society expects children to just miraculously recover from these traumatic events. Often the symptoms and emotions of trauma are deeply repressed, leaving the children unaware yet emotionally vulnerable. Recovery involves healing the psychological harm by helping to establish safety, acknowledging the trauma, resolving the loss and grief, and ultimately supporting the restoration of interpersonal connections.

The therapeutic alliance is critical in the early phases of trauma work with adolescents, however challenging it may be to develop. Teens frequently deny that they need the help of a therapist. They deny the existence of their problems. To complicate matters further, their parents have little information about the trauma their child may have experienced. So the parents themselves may be reluctant to engage in a therapeutic relationship, because they may not see the need. Their reluctance is also shadowed by their deepest internalized fears: what I have read is true; the social worker was right about the possibility of early harm; and how can I parent a child who has experienced so many bad things?

Our experience in working with hundreds of later-placed children, has shown us that the majority of teens have experienced some form of emotional, physical, and or sexual trauma. To negate or avoid this prevalence is not therapeutically acceptable when choosing to work with this population. These are children who have been betrayed by adults and whose trust has been violated. At their deepest core they feel a sense of helplessness and terror. Those who were supposed to have taken care of them were the same individuals who imposed physical violation or injury, emotional upheaval, or committed abusive or violent acts in front of them. Worse yet, while they may have been removed from abusive parental situations, many experience more abuse by the person or persons who are supposed to be safe caretakers.

In her book *Playing Hard at Life: A Relational Approach to Treating Multiple Traumatized Adolescents*, Etty Cohen (2003) explores several tenets to building a strong therapeutic alliance when dealing with traumatized adolescents. Mirroring our work, she speaks strongly that the therapists' emotional responsiveness is crucial, most importantly their expression of tenderness. Cohen refers to a quote by Ferenczi (2003, 114) that poignantly states,

> *Patients cannot believe that an event really took place, or cannot fully believe it if the analyst as the sole witness of the event persists in his cool, unemotional, purely intellectual attitude, while the events are of a kind that must evoke, in anyone present emotions of revulsion, anxiety, terror, vengeance, grief and the urge to render immediate help: to remove or destroy the cause or the person responsible, and since it is usually a child, an injured child, who is involved, feelings of wanting to comfort it with love.*

Kenrick (2004) in her work at Tavistock Clinic, also stresses the need for the therapist to provide a holding environment. She also describes the therapist's need to tolerate the child's anger. Tubero (2002) describes the reenactment of attachment issues in the therapeutic relationship.

We have found that with tenderness, validation and nurturance we can create an atmosphere that affords teenagers the possibility of giving themselves the permission to experience repressed feelings, thoughts, and memories tied to years of loss and trauma. With permission, the feelings can come to the forefront of consciousness. It is this carefully constructed atmosphere of mutual respect and tenderness that opens the locked doors where their deep pain and sorrows lie. The therapist's nurturance and nonjudgmental acceptance is crucial if healing is to occur. We must go to a place that can be uncomfortable, unbelievable, and unexplainable. Talking and giving permission to explore the past allows teens to connect with traumatic events, which they would not otherwise do.

Beyond the therapeutic relationship, the most essential ingredient for recovery is the emotional support by the family, which will assist in the rebuilding of self and the possibility for rebuilding safe connections to others. The establishment of reconnections is tenuous as the adolescent may have lived in environments where adults betrayed them, thwarted a basic sense of trust, fostered unpredictable living situations, and severed attachments. The teen's concept of parent/caretaker is built upon a harming relationship, not one of safety, love, and stability.

In *Trauma and Recovery* (1992), Judith Herman strongly purports that recovery from trauma can only take place in the context of relationships. She discusses how the survivor must recreate the psychological bases for trust, autonomy, identity, and intimacy that have been damaged by the traumatic event. The reestablishment of these psychological tasks must be reformed through relationships — albeit with the therapist and the adoptive family.

● ●

CASE EXAMPLE

Jasmine, age seventeen, was removed from her biological family at the age of seven after being found with her two brothers in an abandoned car. She and her siblings were placed in the care and custody of a local child welfare agency. Following an investigation in which child abuse and neglect was substantiated, the children were placed into foster care. After living in several placements Jasmine was placed for adoption at age of eleven. Jasmine entered therapy six years after placement because she was unable to develop a strong bond with her adoptive parents and was asking to be removed from their home.

Jasmine presented as guarded and well defended, and reported that there were not any problems other than she did not want to live with "these" people anymore, and wanted out! Jasmine was strongly holding on to a glorified picture of her birth mother and fantasized about being reunited with her. She was extremely skilled at pushing others away, including her previous three therapists. Jasmine engaged in therapy like a tiger waiting for the kill. She took every opportunity to lash out at the therapist and find reasons to test distrust and challenge the therapeutic relationship.

Jasmine slowly calmed down in therapy and guardedly began to join in the therapeutic relationship. The therapist continued to create a sense of safety for her client, building a fragile alliance between herself and Jasmine. Following a very confrontational session with her family, Jasmine blurted out, "The abuse in this family is no different from the abuse in my birth family." Jasmine went on to explain that she didn't see much difference between verbal abuse and physical abuse. "It's all abuse in my mind!" The therapist asked Jasmine to tell her about what happened in her birth family. After much silence, Jasmine's affect shifted. She became sullen and lifeless, and exuded a sense of emptiness. In an emotionless way she recounted her memories. She shared that she was thrown against walls, pulled by her hair, locked in closets, hit, deprived of food, and sometimes touched in a bad way by her stepfather. Jasmine looked helplessly at the therapist waiting for some judgment call and reason to thwart this intimate exchange. At the same time, she was desperately hoping for someone to listen to her words and hold her pain in a tender, loving way. "Nurturance and love is the core of what will heal them" (Cohen, 2003).

Beyond establishing nurturance, the therapist must be able to join with the adolescent and accept the journey of rewitnessing the traumatic events and acknowledging the injustice of what has occurred. One must help the adolescent to regain a sense of control by empowering them as active agents of change. The issue of control in this discussion is like an octopus. All victims of abuse will communicate the power of the abuser and loss of control they felt throughout the trauma experience.

For adopted adolescents, the issue of control is experienced on an additional level. Although they are happy they were adopted, they never had a say in one of the most important decisions of their lives. For the later-placed teen, this issue also holds true. Jasmine was very clear in her early sessions that even though she was eleven and the judge asked her if she wanted to be adopted, she felt railroaded into the decision. "I didn't really want to be adopted, not after all the things that had happened in my life. I don't trust anybody, but my brothers were also to be adopted. If I had said no, I would have probably ruined it for them. Some choice I had." Control also plays a major role in the development of adolescents. It is at this key stage in their lives that feeling and being in control is like winning the gold medal in the Olympics. It is what teenagers live and breathe for — control of one's life.

Jasmine began to question how adults could be so cruel and expressed rage toward her stepfather. "If I could I would kill him for what he did to me; I hate him." For the first time in therapy, the stark, controlled composure softened and tears began flowing down her cheeks. "I have never told anyone this before; I mean, those social workers knew what happened because they took me away, but not all those other people. Everyone thinks they know what happened but I never really wanted them to know — I didn't want to talk about it. Why am I talking about it now?" Jasmine was talking about it now because she had found a person she could trust, a person who understood the issues and could tolerate sitting with her in all of her pain. Trust — a word we use so loosely, but to these teens it is precious and rare. Jasmine trusted no one. Being let down by yet one more adult was something she could not bear.

The therapy shifted to supporting Jasmine as she began to mourn the losses associated with the trauma she had revealed. We know that grief shared is grief diminished (Lewis, 1976). As therapists working with children and teens who have experienced profound trauma, we must sit with their pain and help them to adequately mourn their losses. One cannot work with trauma victims without moving into grief work. It was not until the therapist guided Jasmine to feel her feelings that she began to further reveal the harm visited upon her. Helping adolescents to recapture their emotions releases them from the realm of emptiness where they have been existing for some time. They can then reconnect with the very part of themselves they have been severed from and begin to heal. As adolescents allow the memories to surface, they are hit by a giant wave of guilt and shame. Trying to make sense of these acts of violation, they believe on some level that they somehow deserved or caused them. It's hard for young people to come to understand how and why the people who were supposed to love and protect them from harm were the very people who caused such harm.

Following this initial disclosure, Jasmine continued in subsequent sessions to reveal more pieces of her traumatic life as a young child. Every step of the way she questioned her part in this horrid story. Her sense of self-worth had been marred by her experiences of abuse. "Why would anyone think that kids like me walk around just loving themselves or loving anyone else? Love has never crossed my heart." The therapist asked Jasmine to think back as far as she could see if there had been any adult whom she could recall being caring toward her. Minutes passed and very sullenly Jasmine said, "My fourth grade teacher. I remember I could count on her when I was being moved from one place to the next." Searching for previous lifelines in a traumatized child's life provides the initial building blocks for future connections. We have found that helping children acknowledge safe connections helps to dispel their entrenched belief system that all adults are harmful and can't be trusted.

Not only did Jasmine continue to divulge to her therapist, she also cautiously began to extend the truths to individuals outside of the therapeutic relationship. One day Jasmine came into session and revealed that she shared some parts of her story with a female friend in her church youth group. She was anxious about this exposure, but she saw this as a big step in her recovery. Jasmine has had many relationships, but none that she could consider being a close friend. She was surprised that this girl was supportive and never questioned what she had shared. Jasmine felt relieved to have finally shared this with someone outside therapy. Although the therapist carefully tried to get her to talk about this with her adoptive parents, Jasmine remained steadfast in not disclosing to them. She still felt extremely vulnerable and believed that in some way they would use this against her in the future. Her trust level was guarded and tenuous at best.

● ●

Working with her family is important at this stage of recovery to help reinforce the severity of the past abuse and provide insight into Jasmine's emotional guardedness as a critical protective device, which she had used for a long time and was not yet willing to release. It is not uncommon for adoptive parents to feel confused and anxious when trauma is revealed. The therapist should consider a few individual sessions with the parents early on in the therapeutic process to explore the role trauma may have played in the teen's life before they joined their family. In our experience the family often had no prior knowledge of trauma. We recommend that the therapist establish a therapeutic alliance with the adolescent first and then integrate conjoint family work.

Although Jasmine's parents had some knowledge of her abuse history, they were quite embedded in hurt and pain as a result of Jasmine's ongoing rejection of them. This dynamic presents itself frequently when working with later-placed teens, who can be emotionally withholding and, at times, punitive toward the very people they secretly want to connect with. Jasmine's parents needed to understand the depth of their daughter's abuse history. They needed education on the psychological ramifications of such prolonged trauma and the origin of the pathology that prevails when one is not given the opportunity to heal from such victimization.

Engaging the family is essential to the healing process, as discussed earlier. This may seem incongruent for those who embrace the theoretical construct that no parent contact should take place when treating teens.

It is the authors' strong position that parents must be involved on some level when treating adolescents who present with high risk-taking behaviors, high acuity of psychological symtomatology, and /or with histories of longstanding abuse, neglect, or deprivation. The therapist in these cases is a tightrope walker — supporting the autonomy of the adolescent and at the same time earning a trusting, cooperative relationship with the parents.

Jasmine's parents, though angry with their daughter for many years of hostile connections, are paramount in her recovery. Jasmine's parents presented as detached, suspicious, and withholding. They complied with therapy; however, they stated that they were reaching their wits' end and were not sure how much longer they could hang on.

"Hanging on" is the way many parents describe parenting children whose lives have been fraught with past abuse and neglect. It is not an easy thing to do. This is how adoptive parent Kathleen Dugan describes it:

As the parent of twelve children, eight of whom are adopted, I thought I was an expert at parenting until I began to adopt older children whose lives were traumatized in ways that I knew nothing about. I soon found out that giving a loving and safe home wasn't even close to what they needed. Their childhoods had been ripped away from them, and for many of my children their belief in good parents was shattered beyond repair. No matter how carefully I choose my words, their perception of what I was saying was misinterpreted. It almost appeared as though they were hearing my words through some sort of fuzzy filter — a filter that only allowed the words 'adults cannot be trusted, I must protect myself no matter what, don't believe what they are saying, they will only hurt you.' No matter what kind of help I sought out no one seemed to have an answer. Through twenty-five years of educating myself and experiencing living with children of abuse I know that a lot of the advice that was given to me was not only incorrect but also harmful in some instances. The trauma that my children lived with indeed needed to be dealt with in order for our family to survive, and survive we have.

The key to our survival was finding therapists who understood how trauma is manifested in children, taking the approach that we as adoptive parents are not to blame — we didn't cause the problem, but we desperately desire to be an integral part of the solution. How can we be responsible for things we never knew about?

REVISITING THE TRAUMA

The incongruence in leading a child and or adolescent to recall painful memories presents a conundrum when we contemplate the process of healing. Our inclination as adults is to protect, shield, or remove the child from painful circumstances. To engage therapeutically in trauma work, therapists must carefully, respectfully, and nonjudgmentally guide adolescents through a process of exploring hurtful, traumatizing experiences. We may ask ourselves how much recall is necessary to recover: Is it better to follow the adolescent's lead or employ a process of skillful probing?

In our experience adolescents' ability to begin to recall the traumatic events falls along a continuum that is built upon sense of safety, trust, and confidence within the therapeutic process. As the trust with the therapist is established, the teen will slowly move along this continuum of disclosure one step at a time. It is a process that cannot be rushed. As one adolescent stated in therapy, "Rome was not built in a day! Why do all you adults think that trust can be built in a day?"

The adolescent's readiness to process trauma does not follow any prescribed time frames. It depends on several factors, such as the adolescent's and therapist's emotional connectedness to the therapeutic relationship, trust in the therapy process, and the teen's motivation for treatment. We have seen adolescents who engage in the process within several months of therapy and others who have taken a few years. Certainly, this type of work cannot and should not be thought of in the context of brief, short-term therapy.

Inherent in most later-placed adoptions is the dilemma of disclosure of abuse that had never been documented and or substantiated. As a result, therapy sometimes feels like walking with blindfolds on, unaware where you are going and stumbling as you try to find your way. Thus the exploration usually proceeds by both following the lead of the adolescent and engaging in carefully guiding probing to further the process of recall. Many adolescents who have experienced trauma skirt the edges of the exploration. They may recall an aspect of the traumatic event but quickly shy away, like a turtle retreating into its protective shell.

● ●

CASE EXAMPLE

Alicia, age seventeen, placed at age eleven from foster care, began discussing in therapy her strong sexual desire for older men. She described a situation in which she was having strong sexual attraction to male teachers, sport coaches, and, most recently, a friend's father during a sleepover party. She shared that she was struggling with a myriad of emotions — guilt, confusion, shame, and intrigue. A week later in therapy she broached the subject again and shared that she had the same reaction to an older male she had seen at a local mall. She felt perplexed by this occurrence yet strongly aware of her desire. Aware that there was suspected abuse, the therapist began to carefully ask her about her past relationships. Alicia began to sob and yelled at the therapist that she was not going to talk about the past. "Why do we have to go back when I am trying to move forward?" Alicia ran out of the therapy session into the waiting room, screaming that she was never going back. With nurturing encouragement she reentered the session and spoke about her lack of readiness to revisit the past. She yelled at the therapist and asked why she thought that going back was helpful. How did she know what would be helpful? How does the therapist know what is right for her? Underlying her anger are potent questions: Can the therapist hold her pain with her, not let it consume her

Beneath the Mask

like a huge tidal wave? Can the therapist accept the truth without judgment when the truth is told?

In the therapeutic relationship, Alicia became enraged when the therapist offered any suggestions or reflections. "How do you know that to be true?" Alicia shouted, "You don't know me!" Under her rage was the deep fear that yet another person would lead her to a terrifying place and abandon her, again leaving her feeling helpless and out of control. The therapist, like it or not, has been cast in the role of rescuer: one who has now been chosen as the bearer of all their rage and who must not fail the youngster. Alicia desperately wished to be rescued from her pain, but feared another situation in which she sensed a loss of control.

Following the difficult session when Alicia ran out, Alicia's mom, who was concerned by her daughter's reactions after the past few sessions, contacted the therapist. The therapist shared with mom that Alicia was having difficulty exploring issues from her past and that it might take a long time to do so. Mom understood the nature of the issues and acknowledged the need to move at a pace congruent with Alicia's emotional readiness. Mom shared with the therapist that Alicia told her father in the car ride home that she didn't like being in therapy today but would go back next week.

●●●●●●●●●●●●●●●●●●●●●●●●●●

The therapist must keep in the forefront that trauma damages the adolescent's ability to engage in a trusting relationship. In Alicia's case, the therapist needed to consider the concept of traumatic transference. Herman (1992, 136) reflects upon a unique characteristic in patients who have suffered from a traumatic syndrome whereby they have a strong visceral reaction to anyone in a position of authority. According to Herman, the traumatic transference reflects on such a primal level the experience of being terrified and feeling helpless in response to the traumatic event.

It is important to consider these dynamics when working with traumatized adolescents as their fury can be biting and vicious. One may wonder, Why in the world am I trying to work with this young person when he fights me all the way? If she doesn't want help, what's the point of spending an hour listening to her hostility? As with Alicia's case, it may be a long time before teens can begin to acknowledge the past abuse that is currently having such impact in their lives. The therapist needs to stay on the course they have charted together and continue to nurture the therapeutic alliance so that the foundation is laid for the grief and trauma work to ensue.

USING A DEVELOPMENTAL FRAMEWORK
When working with children, no matter what the clinical issues may be, one must proceed within a developmental framework. In her book *Treating Traumatized Children* (1996, 5), Beverly James refers to developmentally sequenced treatment when working with trauma. The premise for this theoretical construct, according to James, is that victims will perceive their trauma differently as they grow and mature. The reworking of the trauma occurs throughout the child's development, and therefore, a mechanism must be in place whereby children and their families are educated about the ongoing nature of this work.

One must not assume that for children who experienced chronic abuse and neglect at very young ages, three months of therapy can help them miraculously recover. Often the initial therapeutic experience only scratches the surface of the depth of the trauma. It may not be until years later, often as a result of a significant life event or transition, that sensory triggers and memories are allowed to break through the realm of unconsciousness.

CASE EXAMPLE

Jennifer was adopted at age seven from a Russian orphanage. She was seen in therapy shortly after placement due to severe temper tantrums that involved physical acting out and aggression. Therapy focused on adjustment issues, helping her and her family to settle in. An adoption assessment was conducted, and there was no information or indication of early abuse. Jennifer's family kept in touch with the therapist over the years and shared that Jennifer was a bright, high-achieving child who did well in school, was compliant at home, and took pride in her academic accomplishments. The temper tantrums had ceased after the initial clinical intervention.

At the age of eighteen, Jennifer attempted suicide by taking an overdose of over-the-counter diet medication. She was assessed at a local emergency room and released because she minimized her intent to kill herself. Her parents contacted the initial therapist and Jennifer was seen. As a result of the earlier relationship with the therapist, Jennifer was more trusting and therefore revealed more than she had in the emergency room. She affirmed the therapist's fears. Jennifer was attempting to kill herself. Jennifer was extremely depressed and wrought with internal strife. She excelled academically, receiving a 4.0 grade point average, but she was socially isolated and withdrawn.

When asked about her school social life, Jennifer shared that she was regularly taunted by peers who called her ugly duckling and made fun of how she dressed. Tears flowed from her eyes and feelings of helplessness consumed her. Jennifer agreed to reengage in therapy and was able to commit to safety with this therapist. She was also seen by a psychiatrist for a medication evaluation because it appeared that a regime of antidepressant medication could help alleviate her depressive symptoms. During the third session, the therapist gained deeper understanding as to why this young woman was so intent in doing the right thing, pleasing everyone around her, and never letting anyone know about her feelings of despair, fear, sadness, and internal rage. Jennifer wrote:

As far back as I could remember, life in the orphanage had its positives and negatives. I loved the freedom the other children and I were given as we progressed in age. I was free to run just about anywhere I pleased as long as I was back at the orphanage before nightfall. I got along well with just about everyone, when I was good that is, and it seemed everything was wonderful. Nonetheless there were just as many negatives as there were positives. There were many times I brought a lot of the fault on myself, such as running away one day because I hated the orphanage. I could not exactly figure out why, but I did and I ran away. A few hours later I ended up going back with two boys from the orphanage. Once I returned, I saw the ladies in front of the doctor's office and my heart sank like a rock, for I knew something bad was going to happen. I fell on the ground and started to have a temper tantrum. The ladies carried me into the doctor's office and gave me a shot and then one of them took me to the girl's dormitory area. I was still screaming and crying. She told me to shut up, and when I would not, she banged my head

Beneath the Mask

against the sink several times. I did not recall what happened afterwards. There were many other times I was beaten. One day several of us decided to rebel and not do anything the lady told us, and of course we got what we deserved. I got the brunt of it since I would not stop having a temper tantrum. The lady beat me with a broom and locked me in the closet for several hours.

As I now look back to those dark memories, my anger boils, and at the same time my sadness engulfs me. As young child I made stupid mistakes that caused my beatings. All I wanted was someone to listen to what I had to say and feel. Someone who cared for me and loved me and I felt none of these feelings I strongly desired. Thus was the reason I possess hatred for the orphanage.

Jennifer had never discussed the abuse she had experienced in the orphanage until she reentered therapy. The verbal trauma she experienced in school triggered all the trauma she had endured in the orphanage. Jennifer shared in therapy that she had been holding this inside for eleven years:

I worried no one would understand. I did not know many people who were adopted as an older child. Most of those kids I knew who were adopted were adopted as infants. How can anyone who has never been through what I have been through understand? I tried to forget. But you know you can't forget your whole life. It's a part of me; it's a part of what happened to me. Because I did not talk about it, it built up more and more of my anger and then one day

*you just lose it and you turn to hurting yourself. I
was so angry and the anger filtered into my life
eleven years later.*

● ●

SELF-HARMING BEHAVIORS AND DISSOCIATION
When treating adolescents who have been victims of childhood trauma, one may see a population that engages in self-harming behaviors, such as cutting and burning. The act of self-harm can be confusing and frightening to those close to the adolescent. In most situations, self-mutilation occurs by using a sharp object — usually a knife, razor, nails, or broken glass — to cut places on the body that are not life threatening. Lighters, lit matches, or lit cigarettes may also be used to inflict self-injurious burns. In his book *Cutting: Understanding and Overcoming Self-Mutilation* (1998, 44), Steven Levenkron helps the reader to understand the reasons for this aversive behavior: "Self-mutilators have many different reasons for their actions and are tormented by a spectrum of feelings." He goes on to delineate that the two primary characteristics which he has encountered in his work among cutters are

1. a feeling of mental disintegration, of inability to think; and

2. a rage that can't be expressed, or even consciously perceived, toward a powerful figure in their life, usually a parent (Levenkron, 1998, 44).

What we have gleaned from the adolescents who are engaging in these types of behaviors is that they learn that the act of inducing physical pain temporarily relieves the flooding of emotional turmoil and pain they experience as a result of early childhood traumas.

Beneath the Mask

CASE EXAMPLE

Lynn, discussed in chapters 4 and 5, has been struggling with cutting for the past five years. Her arms and hands are scarred by years of self-mutilation to the point that she often needs to wear long-sleeved shirts when in public places. It is hard for us to understand why an adolescent would seek such ongoing pain to relieve the emotional suffering.

Lynn's cutting offered soothing relief to her painful psychological conflict. She described feeling disconnected from her parents, her peers, and herself. As her feelings of disconnection surged, Lynn would experience what Levenkron (1998) terms *mental disintegration*. Lynn's cutting served to help ground herself and helped her feel less fragmented.

In her early treatment, Lynn presented with a lack of emotional perceptiveness, both internally and externally. She consistently evaluated her self-worth, always coming up short. She felt that she did not deserve to be rescued by the missionaries and should have been left to die. Her rage toward her birth parent remained potent yet repressed. Lynn's emotional pain had no boundaries; it had an infinite life of its own. Lynn described her cutting as calming. "It helps me come back. I feel calm, the pain has a beginning and an ending. People don't know what it is like to live with so many intense painful thoughts. They don't go away — unless, of course, I cut. I wish I was not adopted. It hurts so much to think that I will never see my mother again. She's dead." Lynn's therapy incorporated expressive therapies — drawing, collage making, writing, and sand tray work — to help her begin to identify what a feeling is, learn how to express her own feelings, and gradually face the sources of these powerful feelings.

● ●

It has been our experience that many of the later-placed children we have worked with consistently exhibit symptoms that appear to be dissociative in nature. However, it is oftentimes difficult to accurately formulate a diagnostic impression of dissociative disorder, as these behaviors tend to be sporadic in frequency and intensity.

The most common symptom we see in our clients is spontaneous trance states. This is evidenced by the young person looking as if they are "spacing out." Their eyes have a blank-stare quality, and there is no eye contact with the therapist. They may lose verbal connection and are clearly not in tune with their surroundings.

Remember the case of Jasmine? She had frequent dissociative episodes in which she would drift into a zoned-out place during exploration of situations that were traumatic. It is important for the therapist to bring this symptom into the adolescents' awareness so that the teen can identify these adaptive mechanisms early on. So, in the case of Jasmine the therapist quickly and gently asked her where she had drifted away to. The therapist said, "Jasmine, I noticed that when we start to talk about the relationship with your birth parents you blank out. Do you know that you are doing this?" Jasmine confirmed for the therapist that indeed she does check out; she says she listens to a song in her head. The therapist asked Jasmine to think about what we could call this so that we can talk about it when it happens again. Jasmine said, "Well I guess you can say I tune out." Who says adolescents don't have a sense of humor?

Luba, adopted from Eastern Europe with her sister, whom we discussed previously in a case example, also exhibited signs of dissociation, particularly when she become overwrought with her grief and

beneath the mask

loss issues regarding the death of her birth parents shortly before she was adopted. During one particular session with her mom present, Luba was talking about the abuse she experienced in her birth family and her confusion surrounding the cruelty of her birth father. Luba quietly checked out, gazing into space, ceasing communication and presenting a somber affect. A few minutes passed and the therapist asked her, "Where did you go? You seemed to leave this room."

Very softly, Luba shared that she was visiting a special place she would go to at the orphanage when she was sad or overwhelmed. When she was asked to describe the place, she said, "It's a beautiful garden behind the orphanage." As she was describing the garden, the therapist handed her a piece of paper and asked her to draw the garden. As she drew, she revealed that when life became unbearable in the orphanage she would sneak out and go to this garden. She described how peaceful this place was for her. That is why she still goes there in her mind when she feels sad, unsafe, or alone.

Luba's mom verified that this garden did exist; she had seen it when they were at the orphanage in one of their earlier visits. The therapist took this opportunity to discuss this not only with Luba but also with her mother, who had been worried about her daughter's daydreaming and distancing behaviors. Mom had not previously understood the garden's importance to Luba.

When dissociation does occur, it presents an opportunity to discover more about where the adolescent goes mentally when the world seems too overwhelming. Once teens can identify and begin to experience the painful feelings associated with the losses, they then can remember the persons, places, or things that are not a part of their lives anymore.

This stage affords young people the ability to finalize and have partial closure to their past. It is at this point that the therapist can safely offer probing questions to aid in this process, just as the therapist asked Luba to describe and then draw her garden. Therapists should encourage youngsters to partially re-experience the place and the associated emotions. Luba's therapist asked her where she sat in the garden — on a rock, on the grass under a tree, in an open space? She was asked to describe what the plants and the trees were like. She was asked what the garden smelled like and what it felt like to sit in the garden — happy sad, lonely, peaceful? Specific, concrete details help the youngster to reexperience crucial events at an emotional level.

THE LENGTHY HEALING PROCESS

Teens placed at older ages who have come from traumatic backgrounds will need a therapeutic setting that can provide intervention services for long periods — even years. Therapy may be sequenced and consist of multiple short-term episodes. Throughout the therapeutic relationship, teens should understand why they are in therapy, what the current goals of the treatment are, and what they will be working on. Therapists should make references to specific achievements that will indicate that this phase of therapy should stop.

We prescribe holding progress meetings with the teen to review their accomplishments along the way. These reviews have proven invaluable to us in our work with teens. The adolescent is often amazed at what they have accomplished. We also identify what work may be left to do in the future. It is important to respect the teen's desire to take a break from therapy. Both the therapist and the adolescent should recognize the clinical gains and support pauses in treatment.

Rarely is final termination of therapy in the adolescent's best interest. An open-door policy is usually more effective. Teens need to know that they can come back at any time they want, and they need to be told that it is likely issues will crop up in the future that they will need to deal with. Carefully laying out potential issues for the future is helpful because it gives kids permission to reenter treatment and normalizes the developmental path trauma takes. Allowing adolescents to have some say in this process fosters a strong sense of control and empowerment. Adolescents also receive a very important message from the therapist that they worked hard during the current phase of treatment.

Treatment of adolescents also requires holding a transition session with the parents. Just as the adolescent must be educated about the life cycle of trauma recovery, so must the parents. Parents need to grasp that new issues will arise as the adolescent matures and that the surfacing of these issues is by no means indicative of clinical failure. Too often parents expect that the first therapeutic intervention will be the last. They need to learn that post-traumatic symptoms may reoccur when teens are faced with stressful situations or when they reach key milestones in their development, such as graduation from high school. Giving permission for teens to focus on the present, leaving the past behind for now, is acceptable and sometimes indicated therapeutically. Parents need to feel at ease with these breaks in therapy and understand their benefit. Therapists may want to engage adolescents in helping to educate their parents about what they learned are their personal triggers and behaviors, which may indicate the need to reengage therapists for support. This process reinforces the task of empowerment of teens and helps them to take responsibility for their recovery. It also affords the creation of a collaborative relationship among all parties — the teen, the parents, and the therapist.

● ● ● ● ● ● ● ● ● ● ● ● ● ● ● ● ● ● ● ●

CASE EXAMPLE

Irina, who shared her Loss Box in chapter 6, made tremendous strides in therapy. Following several progress review meetings, some including her parents, a consensus was reached that it was time to take a break from therapy; Irina had been seeing her therapist for two years, sometimes twice a week. The therapist held a temporary closure session in which a retrospective clinical review was conducted. Irina left feeling proud of herself and confident that she had the critical coping skills needed to face any challenges of reoccurring post-traumatic symptoms. She was given full permission by her therapist and her parents to contact the therapist and come in for a session at any time.

Several months passed and Irina requested a session. She sat down feeling comfortable and at ease, and stated that there were a few more things she felt she needed to talk through. She requested to resume therapy. She explained that she was having some strong emotions about the abuse she endured by her birth father. Irina has become a very spiritual young woman and said she had been praying about her conflicts, which led her to come back. For the next few weeks, Irina came to therapy dressed very maturely and carrying a list of issues she prepared prior to the sessions.

In one particular session Irina vented her surging rage toward her birth father, something she could not do in prior sessions. She acknowledged how very sad and confused she was now that she has seen what it is like to be nurtured and cared for by loving, responsible parents.

She was conflicted by her anger and at times felt guilty for harboring such rage. She wished to move to a place of Christian forgiveness but felt that she had to allow her feelings to surface. She needed to let go of any responsibility she held on to and wanted someone to listen without judgment to the horror she experienced: the feelings of hunger, the fear of not finding food for her and her sister, the embarrassment of stealing scraps of food from tables or digging through garbage, the fear of violence both witnessed and experienced. At one point in the session Irina looked at the office door and began speaking to her father as if he had walked in the room. She told him how she felt and questioned how he could be so hurtful to herself, her sister, and her mother.

Irina continues to attend therapy following a period of time off. Currently she comes once a month. She continues to bring her list of issues to discuss. The focus of therapy is now much more in the present. Irina uses her time with the therapist as a time to reflect on her life and seek support for any challenges that may arise. She is acutely aware that her past will always be a part of her life but no longer consumes her every waking hour. She has found peace and love in her family. She is free to feel safe in her family and dream about her future. One day she hopes to be an astronaut. Talk about finally flying free!

● ● ● ● ● ● ● ● ● ● ● ● ● ● ● ● ● ● ● ●

Healing is a process and not a one-time event. "The course of therapy does not follow a simple progression but often detours and doubles back reviewing issues that have already been addressed many times in order to deepen and expand the survivor's integration of the meaning of the experience" (Herman, 1992, 213). As we saw with Irina, the impact of early life experiences resonate at different levels during different times; sometimes they resonate with a loud roar, sometimes with a faint tone only the teen can hear.

We must remember when we extend our clinical practices to those children who have histories of loss of loved ones, separation from significant others, physical/sexual abuse, and violence that there is no expiration date on memories. Since the memories don't expire, the relationship between client and therapist should not either. The therapist strives to help adolescents achieve a sense of control over those traumatic events by acknowledging the past, embracing the future, and leaving the door open for teens to leave and reenter as they feel the need.

The therapeutic work discussed in this chapter is difficult, challenging, and at times traumatizing to the therapist. Holding the adolescent's grief, suffering, and emotional pain can be daunting. Facing their distrust, anger, and resistance can be exhausting and frustrating. It is imperative that those of us who engage in this work take care of ourselves and develop appropriate supervision and clinical supports. Most importantly, we must never lose sight of the contribution we can make in the lives of those children who trust enough to invite us along their journey to healing.

afterword

We have tried to convey some of our experiences with adopted adolescents in order to share our thoughts, triumphs, and tribulations with other therapists who may work with this population. We are hopeful that we have communicated our respect for these incredibly brave teens and their parents. Together they face a challenging journey — the fascinating but daunting trip through one of the most trying periods of life. This book is a tribute to the teens and parents whose lives we have had the opportunity to embrace.

The richness of the life experience and the psychological growth that accompanies the synthesis of the complexity of adolescence and adoption creates a unique human being. The teens we treat often emerge from therapy with a depth and creativity beyond expectation. Often the journey ends in triumph!

Given the triumphs, one should not underestimate the difficulty of the journey for many adopted adolescents. As you have joined us on this arduous journey, we hope you have come to agree that adoption is a circumstance of emotional importance in the life of the adolescent and should not be ignored. Our primary emphasis has been on the approaches that seem helpful in allowing adolescents and their families to explore the unique issues inherent in adoption. We have described some of the techniques that have been beneficial to our clients as they come to grips with the complex issues created by the collision of the circumstance of being adopted and the demands of identity formation and emancipation. We believe that some of the most critical processes are grieving relinquishment, understanding the reasons for the adoption, coping with the complexity of multiple parents, and processing past traumatic events.

Of course, the parents must accompany the youngsters as they stumble down all these byroads, doing their best to offer guidance and succor. We hope we have conveyed the profound respect we have gained for the determination and wisdom they bring to the task and the importance of engaging them in the therapeutic journey, for parents of adopted teens must go the extra mile. Parenting by adoption does present challenges that differ from parenting birth children. As with treating most teens, there is that initial resistance, which is not uncommon and must be addressed properly. However, once successfully engaged, this population tends to provide intelligent, well-educated, and highly motivated partners in the therapy endeavor.

The therapist learns much in the process of guiding the shared search. Almost none of the adolescents are dull, predictable, or nonengaging. Almost none of the parents are detached or unwilling to look at their feelings. These families tend to be lively, complicated, and multilayered. It is a privilege to join their fascinating journey.

Writing this book has affirmed our conviction that there must be clinical settings that foster adoption-competent mental health services. This is a growing population. In the United States, more than 1.5 million children are adopted, which represents more than 2 percent of all children in the United States. We feel optimistic that our readers will be stimulated by this discussion and choose to continue

BENEATH THE MASK

to expand their knowledge in regard to treating those whose lives have been touched by adoption.

We began this particular journey with some writing by our clients, and we would like to end this way as well. Sarah entered therapy at age fourteen tormented by rejection and identity confusion, wearing the many masks she'd created to keep others from getting too close. Eventually, the masks were lifted and beneath them was an articulate, bright, engaging young woman who finally found her way out of a web of confusion. After two years of therapy, Sarah wrote this poem for her mother.

LOCKED
BY sarah age 16

You took on a task
Complex and confusing
A locked box with no key
The contents a cup with no handle
No way to pour out what was inside
A diary written inside out
No code to decipher the stories
You took me on
A lonely child with no knowledge of her contents
And you gave her a key
A handle and a code
And now the box is open
The cup poured
And the diary read.

appendix a

figures

FIGURE 4.1
Artwork — Poster

FIGURE 4.2
Artwork — Poster

FIGURE 4.3

Shante's Mask — Before

FIGURE 4.4

Shante's Mask — After

FIGURE 6.1

Rachael's Puzzle

FIGURE 6.2

Irina's Loss Box

Beneath the Mask

FIGURE 6.3
Darin's Loss Box

FIGURE 6.3A – Birth Mom
and Favorite Foster Dad

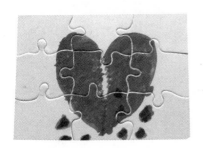

FIGURE 6.3B – Heart Puzzle
Written on Back:
"My Heart is Broken"

FIGURE 6.3C

Darin commemorated these losses: his second foster mom's spaghetti and meatballs, a pet dog, a grandfather who passed away, the baseball his biological sister gave him before their separation, and baseball games and hot dogs with his third foster family.

Appendix B

Resources

ORGANIZATIONS

American Academy of Adoption Attorneys (AAAA)
P.O. Box 33053
Washington, DC 20033
Phone: 202-832-2222
E-mail: webmaster@adoptionattorneys.org
Web site: http://www.adoptionattorneys.org/

AAAA is a national membership association of attorneys who practice, or have otherwise distinguished themselves, in the field of adoption law. AAAA works to promote the reform of adoption laws and to disseminate information on ethical adoption practices. Their membership directory, including members from the United States and Canada, lists attorneys who are well versed in the complexities of adoption law as well as interstate and international regulations regarding adoption.

Association of Administrators of the Interstate Compact on
the Placement of Children (ICPC)
American Public Human Services Association
810 First Street, NE
Suite 500
Washington, DC 20002-4267
Phone: 202-682-0100
Fax: 202-289-6555
E-mail: icpcinbox@APHSA.org
Website: http://icpc.aphsa.org

The ICPC is a uniform state law establishing a contract among party states to ensure that children placed across state lines receive adequate protection and services. The primary function of the ICPC is to protect the interests of both the children and the states by requiring that certain procedures be followed in the interstate placement of children who are being adopted, placed with relatives, or going into residential care of foster family homes.

Casey Family Programs
1300 Dexter Avenue North
Third Floor
Seattle, WA 98109-3542
Phone: 206-282-7300
Fax: 206-282-3555
Toll-Free: 1-800-228-3559
E-mail: info@casey.org
Website: http://www.casey.org

Casey Family Programs provides an array of services for children and youth, with foster care at its core. Casey services include adoption, guardianship, kinship care, and family reunification. Casey is also committed to helping youth in foster care make a successful transition to adulthood.

Children's Bureau (CB)
330 C Street, SW
Room 2412
Washington, DC 20447
Phone: 202-690-6782
Fax: 202-690-5600
Web site: http://www.acf.hhs.gov/programs/cb/

The CB, the oldest federal agency for children and families, is located within the Department of Health and Human Services' Administration for Children and Families, Administration on Children, Youth and Families. The bureau is responsible for assisting states in the delivery of child welfare services designed to protect children and to strengthen families. The bureau provides grants to states, tribes, and communities to operate a range of child welfare services, including child protective services, family preservation and support, foster care, adoption, and independent living:

Child Welfare Information Gateway
Administration of Children, Youth and Families
1250 Maryland Ave, SW
Eighth Floor
Washington, D.C. 20024
Email: info@childwelfare.gov
Web site: www.childwelfare.gov

A service of the Children's Bureau, Administration for Children and Families, U.S. Department of Health and Human Services, we provide access to print and electronic publications, websites, databases, and online learning tools for improving child welfare practice, including resources that can be shared with families. Child Welfare Information Gateway consolidates and builds upon the services formerly provided by the National Clearinghouse on Child Abuse and Neglect Information (NCCANCH) and the National Adoption Information Clearinghouse (NAIC).

Child Welfare League of America (CWLA)
Headquarters
440 First Street, NW
Third Floor
Washington, DC 20001-2085
Phone: 202-638-2952
Fax: 202-638-4004
E-mail: webweaver@cwla.org
Web site: http://www.cwla.org

The CWLA is the oldest national organization serving vulnerable children, youth, and their families. CWLA provides training, consultation, and technical assistance to child welfare professionals and agencies while also educating the public on emerging publication, conferences, and teleconferences. CWLA shares information on emerging trends, specific topics in child welfare practice (family foster care, kinship care, adoption, positive youth development), and federal and state policies.

Collaboration to AdoptUSKids
Adoption Exchange Association
8015 Corporation Drive
Suite C
Baltimore, MD 21236
Phone: 410-933-5700
Fax: 303-933-5716
Toll-Free: 1-888-200-4005
E-mail: info@adoptuskids.org
Web site: http://www.adoptuskids.org

The Children's Bureau funds "The Collaboration to AdoptUSKids" (the Adoption Exchange Association and its partners) to devise and implement a national adoptive family recruitment and retention strategy, operate the AdoptUsKids Web site, encourage and enhance adoptive family support organizations, and conduct a variety of adoption research projects. The collaboration includes Child Welfare League of America (www.cwla.org), Northwest Adoption Exchange (www.nwae.org), Adoption Exchange Education Center (www.adoptex.org), University of Texas School of Social Work and Center for Social Work Research (www.utexas.edu/ssw/#top) and Holt International Children's Services (www.holtintl.org).

Dave Thomas Foundation for Adoption
4150 Tuller Road, Suite 204
Dublin, OH 43017
Phone: 1-800-ASK-DFTA
Fax: 614-766-3871
E-mail: adoption@wendys.com
Web site: http://www.davethomasfoundationforadoption.com/
The vision of the Dave Thomas Foundation for Adoption is that "every child will have a permanent home and a loving family." The foundation strives to make the vision a reality by funding various national initiatives that directly affect waiting children and by expanding the public's awareness of adoption.

Evan B. Donaldson Adoption Institute
525 Broadway
6th Floor
New York, NY 10012
Phone: 212-925-4089
Fax: 775-796-6592
E-mail: info@adoptioninstitute.org
Web site: http://www.adoptioninstitute.org/
The Adoption Institute seeks to improve the quality of information about adoption, to enhance the understanding and perception about adoption, and to advance adoption policy and practice.

Families for Russian and Ukrainian Adoption (FRUA)
PO Box 2944
Merrifield, VA 22116
Phone: 703-560-6184
Fax: 413-480-8257
E-mail: infor@frua.org
Web site: http://www.frua.org/
FRUA is an international parent support network for families who have adopted or are in the process of adopting from the former Soviet Union, Romania, Bulgaria, Hungary, Poland, and other eastern European countries. FRUA is not an adoption agency, nor do they place children.

Joint Council on International Children's Services (JCICS)
1403 King Street
Suite 101
Alexandria, VA 22314
Phone: 703-535-8045
Fax: 703-535-8049
E-mail: jcics@jcics.org
Web site: http://www.jcics.org/
The JCICS is the world's oldest and largest affiliation of licensed, nonprofit international adoption agencies. JCICS membership also includes parent groups, advocacy organizations, and individuals who have an interest in intercountry adoption. JCICS member agencies subscribe to established standards of practice designed to protect the rights of children, birth parents, and adoptive parents.

Kinship Center
124 River Road
Salinas, CA 93908
Phone: 1-800-4-KINSHIP (800-454-6744)
Fax: 831-455-4777
E-mail: info@kinshipcenter.org
Web site: http://www.kinshipcenter.org

Kinship Center is dedicated to supporting the creation and preservation of foster, adoptive, and related families for children who need them. Since 1984, Kinship Center has helped create and support families for thousands of children who could no longer remain safely with their birth parents. Over the years the agency has identified a variety of specific needs to support permanent families for children and has created programs to meet those needs. Today, the agency offers education, mental health and developmental services, counseling, and other post-placement support services to nurture success in children and families.

Korean American Adoptee Adoptive Family Network (KAAN)
P.O. Box 5585
El Dorado Hills, CA 95762
Phone: 916-933-1447
E-mail: KAANet@aol.com
Web site: http://www.KAANet.com/

The central mission for the KAAN is to network groups and individuals related to Korean adoptions. KAAN facilitates dialogue, promotes resource sharing, and disseminates information. KAAN works with its members, the Korean American community, and the Korean government to promote awareness of Korean adoption issues and develop programs that will benefit both the adoption and Korean communities.

Korean Focus for Adoptive Families
1906 Sword Lane
Alexandria, VA 22308
E-mail: info@koreanfocus.org
Web site: http://www/koranfocus.org

Korean Focus is a support organization for families with children from Korea. Korean Focus provides families, adoptees, adoptive parents, and birth parents touched by Korean adoption with information and programs on Korean culture and the adoption experience. Korean Focus is nonprofit, parent-directed, and agency independent.

National Resource Center for Foster Care and Permanency Planning (NRCFCPP)
Hunter College School of Social Work
129 East 79ᵗʰ Street
New York, NY 10021
Phone: 212-452-7053
Fax: 212-452-7475
E-mail: gmallon@hunter.cuny.edu
Web site: http://www.hunter.cuny.edu/socwork/nrcfpp/

The NRCFCPP is funded by the Children's Bureau of the U.S. Department of Health and Human Services. Its mission is to provide information, training, and technical assistance on permanency planning for children in foster care. The center addresses permanency planning issues through policy analysis, research, and information dissemination.

Beneath the Mask

National Resource Center for Special Needs Adoption
16250 Northland Drive
Suite 120
Southfield, MI 48075
Phone: 248-443-0306 or 248-443-7080
Fax: 248-443-7099
E-mail: nrc@nrcadoption.org
Web site: http://www.nrcadoption.org

The National Resource Center for Special Needs Adoption assists states, tribes, and other federally funded child welfare agencies improve their ability to ensure the safety, well-being, and permanency of abused and neglected children through adoption and post-legal adoption services, program planning, and policy development. The center, which believes every child is adoptable and every child deserves a permanent family, provides training, consultation, and informational materials for professional, organization, and parents. The center is a service of the Children's Bureau of the U.S. Department of Health and Human Services.

North American Council on Adoptable Children (NACAC)
970 Raymond Avenue
Suite 106
St. Paul, MN 55114
Phone: 651-644-3036
Fax: 651-644-9848
E-mail: info@nacac.org
Web site: http://www.nacac.org

Founded by adoptive parents, the NACAC is committed to meeting the needs of waiting children in the foster care system and the families who adopt them. The Council advocates the right of every child to a permanent, continuous, nurturing, and culturally sensitive family, and presses to the legal adoptive placement of any child denied that right.

U.S. Department of Health and Human Services, Adminis-
tration for Children and Families (ACF/HHS)
200 Independence Avenue, SW
Washington, DC 20201
Phone: 202-619-0257
Fax: 1-877-696-6675
Web site: http://www.acf.hhs.gov/

HHS is the government agency responsible for protecting the health of Americans. Although the Web site (http://www.hhs.gov) covers a much broader range of health issues, the ACF is devoted to families and children and specific populations, such as minorities and the disabled.

PERIODICALS

Adoption Today *magazine*
Published by Louis &Co. Publishing,
541 E. Garden Dr. Winslow, CO 80550
www.adoptinfo.net
For Families raising children through adoption

Adoptive Families *magazine*
Published by Susan Caughman,
39 West 37th, 15th Floor, New York, NY 10018
www.adoptivefamilies.com
For Families raising children through adoption . For professionals seeking adoption information.

Fostering Families Today *magazine*
Published by Louis & CO. Publishing,
541 E. Garden Dr. Windsor, CO 80550
www.fosteringfamiliestoday.com
For families and professionals affiliated with foster care.

BOOKS ABOUT ADOPTION

For Parents and Professionals

Brodzinsky, David, Schechter, Marshall, and Henig, Robin. *Being Adopted: The Lifelong Search for Self*, 1992.

Eldridge, Sherrie. *Twenty Things Adopted Kids Children Wish Their Adoptive Parents Knew*, 1999.

Fahlberg,Vera. *A Child's Journey through Placement*. 1991.

Gulden, Holly and Bartels-Rabb, Lisa. *Real Parents, Real Children: Parenting the Adopted Child*, 1993.

John, Jaiya. *Black Baby, White Hands: A View From the Crib*, 2001.

Keefer, Betsy and Schooler, Jayne. *Telling the Truth to Your Adopted or Foster Child: Making Sense of the Past*, 2000.

Keck, Gregory and Kupecky, Regina. *Parenting the Hurt Child: Helping Adoptive Families Heal and Grow*, 2002.

Melina, Lois. *Making Sense of Adoption: A Parent's Guide*, 1989.

Raising Adopted Children: Practical, Reassuring Advice for Every Adoptive Parent, 1998.

Melina, Lois and Kaplan, Sharon. *The Open Adoption Experience*, 1993.

Pavao, Joyce Maguire. *The Family of Adoption*, 1998.

Pertman, Adam. *Adoption Nation: How the Adoption Revolution Is Transforming America*, 2000.

Rosenberg, Elinor. *The Adoption Life Cycle: The Children and Families Through the Years*, 1992.

Rosenberg, Shelley. *Adoption and the Jewish Family:Contemporary Perspectives*, 1998.

Wolff, Jana. *Secret Thoughts of An Adoptive Mother*, 1997.

For Children

Cain, Barbara. *Double Dip Feelings*, 1990 (ages 2 and up).

Curtis, Jamie Lee. *Tell Me Again About the Night I Was Born*, 1996 (ages 2-8).

Brodzinsky, Anne. *The Mulberry Bird*, 1996 (ages 7-12).

Freudberg, Judy and Tony Geiss. *Susan and Gordon Adopt a Baby*, 1986 (ages 2-8).

Girard, Linda. *Adoption is for Always*, 1986 (ages 6-12).

Kasza, Keiko. *A Mother for Choco*, 1992 (ages 2-8).

Katz, Karen. *Over the Moon: An Adoption Tale*, 1997 (ages 2-6).

Keller, Holly. *Horace*, 1991 (ages 2-8).

Kroll, Virginia. *Beginnings: How Families Come to Be*, 1994 (ages 4-8).

Livingston, Carole. *Why Was I Adopted?* 1990 (ages 7-12).

Pellegrini, Nina. *Families Are Different*, 1991 (ages 4-8).

Simon, Norma. *All Kinds of Families*, 1976 (ages 2-8).

Schoettle, Marilyn. *W.I.S.E. Up! Powerbook*ˢᴹ, 2000 (ages 6-12) — available also through C.A.S.E.

works cited

Bion, W.R. 1962. *Live company*. London and New York: Tavistock/Routlege.

Blos, P. 1963. *On Adolescence*. New York: The Free Press of Glencoe, Macmillan.

Boss, P. 1999. *Ambiguous loss: Learning to live with unresolved grief*. Cambridge, MA: Harvard University Press.

Bowlby, J. 1969 *Attachment and loss, Vol. 1: Attachment*. New York; Basic Books.

Bowlby, M. 1978. *Family theory in clinical practice*. New York: Jason Aronson.

Bourguignon, J. and Watson, K. W. June 1987. *After adoption: A manual for professionals working with adoptive families.* Springfield, IL: Illinois State Department of Children and Family Services.

Brodzinsky, A.B. 1996. *The Mulberry Bird.* Indianapolis: Perspective Press.

Brodzinsky, D.M. and Schechter, M.D. 1990. *The psychology of adoption.* New York: Oxford University Press.

Brodzinsky, D.M., Schechter, M.D, and Henig, R.M. 1993. *Being adopted: The lifelong search for self.* New York: AnchorBooks, Doubleday.

Brodzinsky, D.M., Smith, D.W., and Brodzinsky, A.B. 1998. *Children's adjustment to adoption: Developmental and clinical issues.* Thousand Oaks, CA: Sage Publications.

Brodzinsky, D.M. and Steiger, C. 1991. Prevalence of adoptees among special education populations. *Journal of Learning Disabilities* 24 (8): 484-89.

Cohen, E. 2003. *Playing hard at life: A relational approach to treating multiply traumatized adolescents.* Hillsdale, NJ: Analytic Press.

Cournos, F. 2004. Parental death and foster care: A personal and professional perspective. *Journal of Infant, Child, and Adolescent Psychotherapy* 3 (3): 342-55.

Crook, M. 2000. *The face in the mirror: Teenagers and adoption.* Vancouver, BC: Arsenal Pulp Press.

Beneath the Mask

Douvan, E. and Adelson, J. 1966. *The adolescent experience*. New York: John Wiley and Sons.

Erikson, E.H. 1956. The problem of ego identity. *J. Amer. Psychoanalytic Society* 4.

Fahlberg, V. 1991. *A child's journey through placement*. Indianapolis: Perspective Press.

Ferenczi, S. 1932. *The clinical diary of Sandor Fenrenczi*. J. Dupont (Ed.) [Translated by M. Balint & N.Z. Jackson, 1988] Cambridge, MA: Harvard University Press.

Fravel, D.L. and Kohler, J.K. 2001. Questionnaire for Psychological Presence as Perceived by parties to Adoption (QP4A, Form D, revised for interview administration with foster children in middle childhood). Available from author.

Freud, A. 1965. *Normality and pathology in childhood: Assessments of development*. New York: International Universities Press.

Friedenberg, E.Z. 1965. *Coming of age in America*. New York: Vintage Books, Random House.

Giedd, J.N., Blumenthal, J., Jeffries, N.O., Castellanos, F.X., Liu, H., Zijdenbos, A., Paus, T., Evans, A.C., and Rappoport, J.L. 1999. Brain development during childhood and adolescence: A longitudinal MRI study. *Nature Neuroscience* 2 (10): 861-63.

Grinker, R.R. 1962. Mentally healthy young males (homoclites). *Archives of General Psychiatry* 6: 405-53.

Grotevant, H.D. and McRoy, R.G. 1998. *Openness in adoption*. Thousand Oaks, CA: Sage Publications.

Gulden, H. and Bartels-Rabb, L. 1993. *Real parents, real children: Parenting the adopted child*. New York: Crossroad Publishing.

Herman, Judith. 1992. *Trauma and Recovery*. New York: Perseus.

Hersch, P. 1996. *A tribe apart: A journey into the heart of American adolescence*. New York: Fawcett Columbine.

Howard, J.A. and Smith, S.L. 2003. *After adoption: The Needs of adopted youth*. Washington, DC: CWLA Press.

Hoxter, S. 1983. Some feelings aroused in working with severely deprived children. In: *Psychotherapy with severely deprived children*, ed. M. Boston & R. Szur. London: Routledge & Kegan Paul.

James, B. 1996. *Treating traumatized children: New insights and creative interventions*. New York: The Free Press.

Jewett, C. 1982. *Helping children cope with separation and loss: Divorce, death, absence, adoption, foster care, sibling loss* (Revised ed.). Cambridge, MA: Harvard Common Press.

Keck, G.C., and Kupecky, R.M. 1995. *Adopting the hurt child: Hope for families with special needs kids*. Colorado Springs, CO: Pinon Press.

Kendler, K.S., Neale, M.C., Kessler, R.C., Heath, A.C., and Eaves, L.J. 1992. Childhood parental loss and adult psychopathology in women: A twin study perspective. *Archives of Gen. Psychiatry* 49 (2): 109-16.

Kenrick, J. 2004. Remembering and forgetting: Working with memories of trauma with fostered and adopted children. *Journal of Infant, Child, and Adolescent Psychotherapy* 3 (3): 356-68.

Kernberg, P.F. 1986. Child analysis with a severely disturbed adopted child. *International Journal of Psychoanalytic Psychotherapy* 2:277-99.

Kirk, H.D. 1964. *Shared fate: A theory of adoption and mental health.* New York: The Free Press of Glencoe.

Kohler, J.K., Fravel, D.L., Whallen, J., Falconier, M. and Riley, D.B. 2001. The psychological presence of birthparents for children in foster care: Implications for concurrent planning. Minneapolis: National Council on Family Relations 63rd Annual Conference.

Kubler-Ross, Elisabeth. 1969. On Death and Dying: New York, Simon and Schuster.

Levenkron, S. 1998. *Cutting: Understanding and overcoming self-mutilation.* New York: Norton & Co., Inc.

Lewis, C.S. 1976. *A grief observed.* New York: Bantam.

Lieberman, M., Yalom, I., and Miles, M. 1973. *Encounter groups: First facts.* New York: Basic Books.

Lifton, B. J. 1994. *Journey of the adopted self: A quest for wholeness.* New York: Basic Books, A Division of Harper Collins Publishers, Inc.

Mathelin, C. 2004. What I hear, I can't write. *Journal of Infant, Child, and Adolescent Psychotherapy* 3 (3): 369-83.

Meeks, J. and Bernet, W. *Fragile Alliance: An Orientation to the Psychiatric Treatment of the Adolescent*, 5th ed. Malabar, FL: Krieger Publishing.

Melina, L. 1989. *Making sense of adoption*. New York: Harper & Row, Publishers, Inc.

Merriam-Webster (Editor). 2001. *Merriam-Webster Collegiate Dictionary*, 10th ed. Springfield, MA: Merriam-Webster, Inc.

Miller, B.C., Fan, X., Grotevant, H.D., Christensen, M., Coyl, D., and van Dulmen, M. 2000. Adopted adolescents overrepresentation in mental health counseling: Adoptees' problems or parents' lower threshold for referral? *Journal of the American Academy of Child and Adolescent Psychiatry* 39, (12): 1504-10.

Munsch, R. 1986. *Love you forever*. Buffalo, NY: Firefly Books.

Nickman, S.L. 2004. The holding environment in adoption. *Journal of Infant, Child, and Adolescent Psychotherapy* 3 (3): 329-41.

Nydam, R. 1999. *Adoptees come of age*. Westminster, KY: John Knox Press.

Offer, D. 1987. The mystery of adolescence. *Adolescent Psychiatry* 14: 7-27.

Pavao, J. 1998. *The family of adoption*. Boston: Beacon Press Books.

Perry, B.D., Pollard, R.A., Blakely, T.L., Baker, W.L., and Vigilante,

D. 1995. Childhood trauma, the neurobiology of adaptation and "use-dependent" development of the brain: How "states" become "traits." *Infant Mental Health Journal* 16: 271-91.

Pynoos, R. and Eth, S. 1985. *Post-traumatic stress disorder in children*. Washington, DC: American Psychiatric Press.

Reitz, M. and Watson, K. 1992a. *Adoption and the family system: Strategies for treatment*. New York: The Guilford Press.

————— and —————. 1992b. Providing services after adoption. *Public Welfare* (Winter), 5-13.

Rosenberg, E. 1992. *The adoption life cycle: The children and their families through the years*. New York: Free Press.

Salamone, F. 2000. Beyond "secrets and lies": Growing up adopted. *Journal of Infant, Child, and Adolescent Therapy* 1 (4): 1-7.

Schoettle, M. 2000. *W.I.S.E Up! Powerbook*. Silver Spring, MD: The Center For Adoption Support and Education Inc.

————— 2003. *S.A.F.E. at School: A manual for teachers and counselors: Support for adoptive families by educators at school*. Silver Spring, MD. The Center for Adoption Support and Education, Inc.

Schore, A.N. 1994. *Affect regulation and the origin of the self: The neurobiology of emotional development*. Mahwah, NJ: Lawrence Erlbaum Associates.

————— 2001. The effects of early childhood trauma on right brain development, affect, regulation, and infant mental health. *Infant Mental Health Journal* 22: 201-69.

Sherick, I. 1983. Adoption and disturbed narcissism. *Journal of American Psychoanalytical Association* 31: 487-514.

Silverman, M.A. 2004. Insecurity and fear of attachment in a troubled adoption: A clinical example. *Journal of Infant, Child, and Adolescent Psychotherapy* 3 (3): 313-28.

Smith, S.L. and Howard, J.A. 1999. *Promoting successful adoptions: Practice with troubled families*. Thousand Oaks, CA: Sage Publications.

Sowell, E.R., Peterson, B.S., Thompson, P.M., Welcome, S.E., Henkenius, A.L., and Toga, A.W. 2003. Mapping cortical change across the human life span. *Nature Neuroscience* 6 (3): 309-15.

Steele, M., Hodges, J. Kaniuk, J. Hillman, S., and Henderson, K. 2003. Attachment representations and adoption: Associations between maternal states of mind and emotion narratives in previously maltreated children. *Journal of Child Psychotherapy* 29: 187-205.

Subramanian, S. 2004. Eileen: Treatment of a foster child. *Journal of Infant, Child, and Adolescent Psychotherapy* 3 (3): 384-90.

Trozzi, M. and Massimini, K. 1999. *Talking with children about loss*. New York: Perigee Books.

Tubero, A. 2002. Adoption, attachment, and re-enactment in the therapeutic setting: A case study of an adolescent girl. *Journal of Infant, Child, and Adolescent Therapy* 2 (1): 39-65.

Verrier, N. 1994. *The primal wound: Understanding the adopted child*. Baltimore: Gateway Press, Inc.

Vorus, N. 2004. Treatment of an adopted child: The case of Roger. *Journal of Infant, Child, and Adolescent Psychotherapy* 3 (3): 391-97.

Zuckerman, J.R. and Buschsbaum, B. 2000. Strangers in a strange room: Transference and Countertransference paradigm with adoptees. *Journal of Infant, Child and Adolescent Psychotherapy* 1 (4): p 9-28.

acknowledgments

Foremost, we would like to show our gratitude to the teens and families who trusted us to join their journey. It is their expressed wish for more professionals to become adoption competent that motivated us to write this book. We also want to thank all the teens and their parents who contributed their personal stories, writings, and artwork that provide a richness to the book that could not have been achieved without their contribution. You are all a very important part of this book. Second, we would like to extend a very special recognition to Kathleen and Michael Dugan, who have dedicated personal and financial commitment to C.A.S.E. Without their support of the creation of a post-adoption center, none of this work could have happened. Their commitment to the children and families we serve is to be commended. We would also like to thank the following individuals for their contribution to this book: Valerie Kunsman, Marilyn Schoettle, Madeleine Krebs, Barbara Franck, Ellen Singer, Daphne Jones and the entire clinical team at C.A.S.E, Mary Jane Kennelly, Andrea Adler, Dr. Philippe Dupont, and the staff at the Developmental School Foundation. A special recognition to Cathy Maloney who helped two very non-computer-competent writers pull this manuscript together. Miracles do happen! A very special thanks to my friend and colleague Barbara Holton for her countless hours in providing sound editorial advice. I would like to recognize Dr. Joyce Maguire Pavao and Sharon Kaplan Roszia; without their pioneering work in the field of post-adoption and long-term guidance, none of this would have ever entered my mind.

I would also like to acknowledge my co-author, who has been my mentor and friend for the past sixteen years, Dr. John Meeks. It is he who provided me with the encouragement and confidence to see myself as an adoptive parent, cheered me on when I was given the opportunity to create C.A.S.E., and has hung in there with me over the past two years as we embarked upon this journey together to write this book. I am honored to join in co-authorship with him.

Finally, I would also like to thank my husband Michael and son Sean for their patience and weekends and evenings without me. Without their support and encouragement and full use of the family office, I may have never gotten past the first few words. I love you both.

glossary
unmasking language

adoptee — An individual who joined his or her family through adoption.

adoption disruption — Refers to the decision of prospective adoptive parents not to proceed with the adoption of a child or teen who has been placed with them for adoption; occurs prior to the legal finalization of the adoption.

adoption dissolution — After the legal finalization of an adoption, the decision made by adoptive parents not to continue parenting their adopted child or teen and to terminate their parental rights, making the child/teen available to be adopted by another family.

birth parent — An individual who voluntarily makes an adoption plan for their child or who has their parental rights terminated by the courts.

closed adoption — Traditional adoption process in which there is no contact or exchange of identifying information at any time during or after the placement process between the parties involved in an adoption, namely the birth parents (and family) and adoptive parents.

domestic adoption — Any adopted child who was born in the United States. The child can be any age under eighteen, and the adoption is facilitated by a private adoption attorney, a private adoption agency, or a public child welfare agency. In the case of the public child welfare agency, the child is adopted after having first been involved in foster care.

identity formation — The psychological process of determining one's personal belief system, values, interests, life goals, and so on.

international adoption — Any adopted child who was born in another country. The adoption is facilitated either by private adoption attorneys or, more typically, through private adoption agencies.

openness and open adoption — Adoption process that involves contact/communication between birth parents and adoptive parents either prior to or post-placement (e.g., exchange of letters, pictures, telephone contact, in-person meetings, etc.) May include full disclosure of identifying information. In some adoptions, adoption becomes a closed one post-placement. In others, some form of contact may continue post-placement. In truly open adoptions, birth family member's relationship with adoptive family becomes like that of extended family members. In some adoptions, the birth family and adoptive family initiate contact at some point in time post-placement, referred to as "opening a closed adoption."

transcultural adoption — An adoptive family in which the adoptive parents' ethnic backgrounds differs from the adopted child(ren);

can occur in both domestic and international adoptions. Some families are both transracial and transcultural.

transracial adoption — An adoptive family in which the adoptive parents and adopted children are of different races; can occur in both domestic and international adoptions.

index

Beneath the Mask

Becca (adoptee), 58, 93–96, 120–21, 122, 152, 158–59
Beginnings (Kroll), 225
Being Adopted (Brodzinsky, Schechter and Henig), 223, 228
"Beyond 'Secrets and Lies'" (Salamone), 233
Bion, W.R., 227
biracial adoptees, 96–97
    See also racism; transracial families
birthday misinformation, 75–76
birth fathers
    anger toward, 199–201
    information about, 73–75
    psychological presence of, 106–7
    secrecy about, 122–24
    See also birth parents
birth mothers, psychological presence of, 106–7, 109–10
    See also birth parents
birth parent puzzle mural, 152–57
birth parents
    adoptive parent's attitude toward, 43–46
    defined, 241
    fantasies regarding, 13–14, 72
    fear of, 17–18, 93–94, 103, 131
    history of, 46
    idealizing of, 11, 23–25
    identification with, 11
    jealousy of, 14–15
    psychological presence of, 106–7
Black Baby, White Hands (John), 224
Blakely, T.L., 232
"blaming" family, 48, 49
"blind" family, 47, 49

Blos, P., 227
Blumenthal, J., 3, 229
books about adoption, 223–24
    for children, 225
    for parents and professionals, 223–24
    reading and discussion, 157–58
    See also periodicals
Boss, P., 35, 87, 106, 227
Bourguignon, J., 228
Bowlby, J., 171–72, 227
Bowlby, M., 227
"Brain Development during Childhood and Adolescence" (Giedd, Blumenthal, Jeffries, Castellanos, Liu, Zijdenbos, Paus, Evans and Rappoport), 229
Brent (adoptee), 53–54
Brodzinsky, A.B., 1, 9, 149, 172, 225, 228
Brodzinsky, D.M., xviii, xix, 1, 9, 32, 113–14, 119, 172, 223, 228
Buschsbaum, B., 2, 31, 50, 234

C
Cain, B., 225
Camille (adoptee), 126–27
C.A.S.E. assessment model
    assessment of adolescent, 48–56
    assessment of adoptive parents, 37–48
    tenets, 34–37
C.A.S.E. (Center for Adoption Support and Education Inc.), xx–xxi, 105–7, 116
Casey Family Programs, 214
Castellanos, F.X., 3, 229

P

"Parental Death and Foster Care"
(Cournos), 228
parental stuck spots, 119–39
   differences, 124–28
   identity, 132–34
   loyalty, 135–39
   missing information, 121–24
   permanence, 129–32
   reasons for adoption, 119–21
Parenting the Hurt Child (Keck
and Kupecky), 224
parents. *See* adoptive parents; birth
parents; parental stuck spots
Parry, B.D., 232
Patrick (adoptee), 42–43
Paus, T., 3, 229
Pavao, J., 35, 119, 122, 224, 232
Pavel, D.L., 231
Pedro (adoptee), 78–79
peer differences, 10, 82–84
   See also differences
Pellegrini, N., 225
periodicals, 223
   See also books about adoption
permanence
   as adolescent stuck spot, 84–90
   as parental stuck spot, 129–32
Pertman, A., 224
Peterson, B.S., 3, 234
Piaget, J., 21
Playing Hard at Life (Cohen),
178–79, 228
poems by adoptees, xxiii, 62, 69–70,
91, 109, 110–11, 167–68, 207
Pollard, R.A., 232
*Post-Traumatic Stress Disorder in
Children* (Pynoos and Eth),
233
pre- and postnatal information,
38–39

preplacement history, 39–41
"Prevalence of Adoptees among
Special Education Popula-
tions" (Brodzinsky and
Steiger), 228
Primal Wound, The (Verrier), 62,
235
"Problem of Ego Identity, The"
(Erikson), 229
progress meetings, 198
Promoting Successful Adoptions
(Smith and Howard), 234
"Providing Services after
Adoption" (Reitz and Wat-
son), 232
Psychological Presence Measure,
106
"Psychological Presence of Birth
Parents for Children in Fos-
ter Care" (Kohler, Fravel,
Whallen, Falconier and
Riley), 231
Psychology of Adoption, The
(Brodzinsky and Schechter),
119, 228
puzzle as metaphor for adoption,
152–57
Pynoos, R., 233

Q

"Questionnaire for Psychological
Presence as Perceived by
Parties to Adoption" (Fravel
and Kohler), 229
questions
   about adoption, 152–57
   indirect, 27–28
   intrusive and hurtful, 160–62

About the Authors

Debbie Riley, LCMFT, and
John E. Meeks, M.D.

Debbie Riley, LCMFT, is the Executive Director of the Center for Adoption Support and Education, Inc. She received her master's degree from the University of Maryland, Department of Family Studies. She has been a practicing marriage and family therapist for twenty-three years, focusing on adolescent mental health, and treating teens in outpatient, inpatient, and community mental health settings. She is the co-founder of Operation Runaway — a unique public/private partnership between one of the country's largest suburban police departments and a community psychiatric hospital.

Since 1993, she has focused exclusively on the field of adoption, creating an innovative post-adoption family support center in the

Washington metropolitan area. Services include a continuum of comprehensive adoption mental health services, education, and support services for the adoption community. Ms. Riley is an accomplished presenter both locally and nationally on adoption issues and writes for various adoption-related publications.

**John E. Meeks, M.D.,** has been a practicing child and adolescent psychiatrist for more than forty-five years. He received his medical degree from the University of Tennessee. He has taught at the University of Texas Southwestern Medical School and the Georgetown University Medical School. He has served as director of several child and adolescent divisions in psychiatric hospitals. He is co-founder and has served as the president and medical director of The Foundation Schools since 1975. The Foundation Schools operate three K–12 schools for students with emotional disturbance.

He has authored several articles on individual and group psychotherapy, behavior disorders of childhood, treatment, of adolescent suicide, adolescent substance abuse, hospitalization and inpatient treatment and adolescent depression. Dr. Meeks is best known for his classic textbook *The Fragile Alliance*; another book on depression, *High Times, Low Times: The Many Faces of Adolescent Depression*; and his most recent publication, *The Learning Alliance*. Dr. Meeks has presented nationally and internationally. In 1998 Dr. Meeks received the prestigious national Schonfeld Award from the American Society for Adolescent Psychiatry for his lifetime contributions to child and adolescent psychiatry.

ABOUT C.A.S.E.

C.A.S.E. is a private, non-profit adoptive family support center. Its programs focus on helping children from a variety of foster care and adoptive backgrounds to receive understanding and support which will enable them to grow into successful, productive adults.

The Center For Adoption Support and Education continues its commitment to provide high-quality, innovative post-adoption services to families from all adoptive experiences. There are many ways to join with C.A.S.E. to celebrate the joys of adoption for every child and family. For more information about C.A.S.E and how you can help, visit adoptionsupport.org.

All C.A.S.E. books are available online or at your favorite bookstore. Quantity discounts are available to qualifying institutions. All C.A.S.E. books are available to the booktrade and educators through all major wholesalers.

For more information, visit:

WWW.ADOPTIONSUPPORT.ORG

ALSO AVAILABLE...

52 Ways to Talk About Adoption
A unique card game for adoptive families. Created by our adoption-competent staff, whose motto is "Talking is good for everyone", this game encourages family discussion of adoption in a playful and interesting way. We hope that you talk, talk, and talk some more while having fun!

Price: US $20.00

W.I.S.E. Up!℠ Powerbook
W.I.S.E Up! Powerbook will help to empower children from ages six to twelve with answers to questions about adoption.

Price: US $15.00
ISBN: 0-911732-0-6

S.A.F.E. at School Manual
S.A.F.E. at School presents five proactive strategies to help teachers and counselors create a positive adoption environment in school: S.A.F.E. is a complete — but simple — tool for addressing the complex topic of adoption in *any* school.

Price: US $25.00
ISBN: 0-9715732-1-4

Purchase C.A.S.E. productions online at:
WWW.ADOPTIONSUPPORT.ORG